How to
DIVORCE
in New York

How to
DIVORCE
in New York

NEGOTIATING YOUR DIVORCE
SETTLEMENT WITHOUT
TEARS OR TRIAL

GRIER RAGGIO
and
MICHAEL STUTMAN

INTRODUCTION BY HENRY H. FOSTER, JR.
AND
DR. DORIS JONAS FREED

ST. MARTIN'S GRIFFIN
NEW YORK

Design by Helene Berinsky

Library of Congress Cataloging-in-Publication Data

Raggio, Grier H.
    How to divorce in New York / Grier Raggio and Michael Stutman.—
Fully rev. and expanded.
        p.   cm.
    Rev. ed. of: Divorce in New York. 1987.
    Include index.
    ISBN 0-312-09273-3 (pbk.)
    1. Divorce—Law and legislation—New York (State)—Popular
works.   I. Stutman, Michael.   II. Raggio, Grier H. Divorce in New
York.   III. Title.
KFN5126.Z9R34   1993
346.74701'66—dc20
[347.4706166]   93-15257
                                                          CIP

First St. Martin's Griffin Edition: June 1997

10   9   8   7   6   5   4   3   2   1

CONTENTS

CAVEAT

No book on family law can substitute for the sound judgment and advice of a competent matrimonial lawyer dealing with the particular facts of the case.

This book cannot give you legal advice tailored to your situation; it can acquaint you with some of the factors lawyers and judges consider in divorce cases. The book is a guide to the issues you must resolve in creating the financial, custody, and support terms of a divorce settlement. Where it's financially possible, we recommend that you have an attorney as your adviser and employee in navigating through to a negotiated or litigated result.

Preface to the 1997 Edition

In 1987 Grier Raggio wrote *Divorce in New York*. We revised that book in 1993 by writing this one, incorporating some of the important changes in the law. The revision was accomplished with invaluable help from paralegals Anne Gore and Michelle Maher, and a legal intern, Todd Sherman. As the project went forward, it became a bigger task than expected. The psychological divorce chapter in the 1987 book was discarded. This chapter had been taken from *Divorce in Washington: A Humane Approach*, by Lowell K. Halverson and John W. Kydd. John, a therapist as well as an attorney, had written that chapter. We, however, are not therapists and could not verify much of that chapter from our own experience. We decided to say only what we felt we personally knew. Lenard Marlow, a good friend and an attorney who does divorce mediation, helped us immensely in the expression of these ideas and his thoughts on mediation formed the basis for that chapter.

We have kept the introduction and historical and policy overview to the 1987 edition written by Henry H. Foster, Jr., and Dr. Doris Jonas Freed. Professor Foster, who died in 1988, and Dr. Freed, who died in 1993, have been giants in the development of the New York matrimonial law for many years, and we wanted their contribution to the book to remain intact.

We present three models for resolving the custody, property, and support issues that often occur at the end of a marriage: adversary litigation in court, settlement through negotiations done primarily by attorneys, and settlement reached by the parties themselves, perhaps with the assistance of a professional mediator. These models overlap, and a court fight, negotiations through attorneys, and direct exchanges between the parties may each be appropriate at different stages of a case. We generally recommend against full-scale litigation and courtroom trials. The litigation process is slow, painful, and often a tragic waste of the spouse's financial resources. But both husband and wife must be willing and able to reach a common ground if negotiations are to succeed, and serious litigation is sometimes necessary.

One premise of this book is that when settlement negotiations are going on, the spouses should be aware of the standards for property division, custody, and support that New York courts would apply if the case went to trial. These standards are a public definition of what is "fair" and they serve as guidelines for negotiated or mediated settlements. Much of this book therefore discusses those rules as embodied in the New York Equitable Distribution Law.

Between the first publication of this book in the summer of 1993 and now, there have been some important changes in the law applied to divorce cases and the standards applied to attorneys who practice matrimonial law.

In November 1993 new rules were issued to regulate attorneys who practice matrimonial law and the courts that hear matrimonial cases. Attorneys must give potential clients a "Statement of Client Rights and Responsibilities." The attorney and the client sign a comprehensive four-page retainer agreement. A copy of this agreement is provided to your spouse and her attorney as part of the financial disclosure. If you decide to change attorneys, your old attorney must turn over your file to your new attorney, whether you owe money to your old attorney or not. If you have a dispute with your attorney about the amount of the fee, you are entitled to demand arbitration to resolve the problem.

Once a case has started, the parties and their attorneys usually meet with a judge within seventy-five days of the start of the lawsuit. At this meeting the judge assigned to the case tries to help the parties and the attorneys determine the fastest and most economical way to get the case settled or ready for trial. A deadline of no more than six months for the completion of discovery (exchange of information about finances and other issues) is established. If your case requires a trial, the judge is supposed to hear the trial on consecutive days.

The area involving the valuation of licenses and practices has become even more confusing and uncertain. In December 1995, the Court of Appeals issued a decision in the case of McSparron v. McSparron. The court held that the value of professional license did not "merge" in the professional practice, but retained its own separate value. As a consequence, in cases involving licenses, professional or otherwise, experts must value the practice and the license separately. The court then divides the value of the license and/or practice between the spouses, and must avoid "double dipping" if maintenance is awarded.

Many agreements and many judgments of divorce, all made before managed care, provide that one spouse must maintain health insurance for the benefit of the other, or the children, and pay for unreimbursed medical expenses. Many of us carry insurance that pays for 100 percent of covered expenses, if a "participating" doctor or hospital renders the treatment. However if the patient goes "out of network" few of the charges are reimbursed. Does the spouse who is providing the insurance have to pay the charges for the doctor chosen by the patient spouse? Is there any obligation on the patient to use network physicians? Thus far these questions have not been answered. If you are currently negotiating a settlement, or in litigation, these concerns must be addressed.

The last three years have seen a tremendous strengthening of child support enforcement mechanisms. For example, failure to pay child support can result in the suspending of any license granted by the State. This includes driver licenses, licenses to practice law or medicine, real estate broker licenses, teacher licenses, barber licenses, etc. The networking of governmental agency computers enables enforcement to be much more effective.

Although matrimonial law is becoming more complicated, at least half of the fifteen thousand divorces granted each year in New York County do not involve an attorney for either party. Courthouse budgets are being squeezed and staffing levels have been greatly reduced. Nonetheless, we have found the people in the county clerk's offices to be extremely generous with their time and advice for persons trying to navigate an uncontested divorce through the judicial system.

For their help with this book, Michael and I especially wish to thank Lenard Marlow, Lorraine Raggio, Jeanette Stutman, Louise Raggio, Anne Gore, Todd Sherman, Michelle Maher, Josh Getzler, and our perceptive editor, Sheila Cavanagh. I also wish to thank Lowell Halverson and John Kydd both for being coauthors with me on the original *Divorce in New York* and for publishing a revised *Divorce in Washington* in 1990, whose success, added to Michael's arguments, led to this publication.

—Grier Raggio and Michael Stutman
April 1997
New York, New York

INTRODUCTION TO THE 1987 EDITION

THIS BOOK provides a roadmap for one traveling through the divorce process. It is written in plain English for divorce clients and their families and friends. It avoids "legalese," gives examples, and provides an accurate account of the divorce process, which often appears meaningless to the layman. Clients, lawyers, mental health professionals, and the general public will benefit from reading it. New York lawyers will find the book helpful to those of their clients who are struggling with the shocks of separation. It offers much insight and information to help them endure the trauma of divorce.

The strength of this book is that it concentrates on the human, psychological, and economic problems involved in divorce and at the same time clarifies the legal problems. Grier Raggio, the coauthor we know best, is an experienced matrimonial and trial lawyer who cares for people and effectively advances his clients' long-term best interests. He is a proponent of planning for the future and working with the present rather than fighting about the past. He is dedicated to protecting the welfare of the children of divorce, who are too often the real sufferers when their parents go to court.

The book provides essential knowledge on property distribution upon divorce, maintenance, child support, custody, and visitation in understandable language for the lay reader.

Mr. Raggio discusses such hotly contested issues as joint custody and has added an interesting chapter on the legal rights of nonmarital partners or cohabitants.

Those rules are discussed here in a practical and realistic way as knowledge the divorcing person needs to participate in settling his or her own divorce problems. There is more emphasis on what goes on behind the scenes in solving those problems than about technical rules applicable to divorce trials, such as the rules of legal procedure and the grounds of divorce in New York. The latter are mentioned, but Mr. Raggio is chiefly concerned with the divorce process as it takes place in real life and in the personal experiences of clients. For many years over 90 percent of New York divorces have been "uncontested." This means that only one party actually shows up in court, and usually there is a ritual inquest with stock questions and answers that may take all of ten minutes. The practical significance of the over nine-to-one ratio of divorce cases that are resolved without a court trial over those that are tried cannot be ignored.

This reality means that for middle- and upper-income clients it is the *negotiation* process that is pivotal: "bargaining leverage" may be crucial. Chapter six gives an insight into the negotiation process and advises the client to concentrate upon what he or she *most* wants and to be prepared to give ground on what the other party *most* wants. Informed predictions of what a court would do in the facts of your case, if there were a trial, often sets limits for negotiation. Mr. Raggio has had considerable experience in negotiation as well as trial work. In passing, it may be of interest that he comes from a family of lawyers. His mother, Louise Raggio of Dallas, is a past chairperson of the Family Law Section of the American Bar Association and remains active in its affairs. His father and two brothers practice in Dallas and are well-known family lawyers. Matrimonial law for the Raggios has been a family specialty.

Of deep concern to Mr. Raggio is the rapidly developing alternative of divorce mediation, in which the parties negotiate directly, with the assistance of a trained mediator, and use their attorneys as advisers and draftsmen rather than as gladiators. Mr. Raggio gives the pros and cons of mediation as a way of reaching a divorce settlement and warns of some of its dangers, but obviously favors mediation for those clients where he believes it will work. His working assumption is that divorce is at the same time the legal killing of a marriage and the start of a new legal, social, and economic relationship between the former spouses. The new relationship is particularly important if there are young children, for the divorced parents will be sharing financial and nurturing responsibilities for their children, attending the same school plays, athletic events, graduations, and weddings for many years. A long, bitter divorce process in which the parties do not come to terms with the resentments and regrets they each carry from the marriage will be a continuing poison in that new relationship; conversely, a mediated settlement may be the best start for that new relationship.

Whether mediation is appropriate or not, one of the most helpful features of this book is that it places divorce in the broad context of a person's life and relates the process to short-term and long-term objectives. A client will learn why it is to his or her best interest to bury hostility along with the dead marriage and to constructively plan for the future.

The client who enters the divorce process should be aware of the possible and the probable. Emotionally mature couples have always been able to agree and reach an amicable settlement, with or without the use of lawyers or mediators. But that civilized behavior is all too rare, and the divorce process often brings out the worst in people, unless the client has listened to a lawyer like Mr. Raggio, who takes a "planning for the future" approach. What the trade calls "bomber" lawyers are easily available; and when a client deliberately chooses a bomber the flak begins, things heat up, bitterness and hostility are intensified, and divorce becomes a life-and-death struggle with no holds barred. Sometimes the bomber snows under his adversary with tons of paperwork, motions, depositions, interrogatories, and the like, in the hope of getting the victim to cry "uncle." Whether the bomber achieves his or her immediate goal or not, inevitably the legal expenses skyrocket and the parties and their children all suffer heavy emotional and psychological casualties.

It need not be that way. From this book you may learn that there are alternatives to a cat-and-dog fight in court where all the dirty linen is exposed and anger is vented. You and your spouse may be fortunate enough to engage attorneys who "cool it" and plan and negotiate effectively for your and your children's futures. Or you and your spouse may be mature and rational enough to go the mediation route, using attorneys only as advisers and draftsmen. Hopefully the tools available in this book will assist you and your spouse to shape your divorce result rather than leaving the job mostly to lawyers and to judges. Even if litigation is necessary, this book can help you in preparing your case and in formulating your long-term goals after divorce. With help and luck you can endure the trauma of the divorce process and become a better person for the experience. As Grier Raggio suggests, set your eyes on the future and bury the past and get on with it so you may make a fresh start. As some of us know, life is too short to be wasted in a running battle to get the better of the person you once loved and who is the parent of your children. Shalom!

—Henry H. Foster, Jr.
Professor of Law Emeritus
New York University

—Doris Jonas Freed, S.J.D.
New York, New York

February 1987

CHAPTER ONE

————— ❖ —————

How to Use This Book

THIS BOOK is written for any person whose marriage is ending. The reality is that one of every two marriages in America ends in divorce. In 1988 alone almost 130,000 New Yorkers had their marriages dissolved by a divorce. We write also for mothers-in-law, brothers, best friends, and others who become emotionally involved in the divorce process.

There are two basic themes in this book. The first is that a fight in court is almost always the wrong way to end a marriage. The second is that husbands and wives should try to take charge of negotiating the essential financial and custody terms of their separation and divorce, either directly with each other or through their attorneys, once it is clear that their marriage is over. With the marriage dead and at least one spouse hurting and bitter, he or she may be tempted to use the courts to punish the other. That is usually not a good idea. There are cases where one spouse has abused and intimidated the other so that direct negotiations between them would be a sham. And violent or fraudulent acts often require going to court immediately rather than negotiating. But such cases remain the exception. We encourage spouses to participate actively in formulating the financial, custody, and support terms of their divorce arrangement.

We also offer help in choosing the right attorney to help

you through to a negotiated, mediated, or litigated settlement. The book's sections on New York law are tools for you to use in evaluating the reasonableness and fairness of any proposed solutions to the specific custody, support, and property division questions in your case. Some of those tools you may not need; for instance, there may be no children, so the child custody portions of the book can be ignored. The entire thrust of the book is to assist you in ending your marriage, if it should be ended, on terms that will best allow you to move forward with your life.

In law school students read cases reporting how judges decide specific disputes. The idea is to learn general principles by studying specific applications. Thus we have created a divorcing couple, Mary Ellen and Jim, using our experiences to illustrate frequent issues in divorce cases. In our example the wife is the economically dependent homemaker and the husband the dynamic businessman. This is not meant to be sexist but is simply a reflection of a common arrangement. Obviously there are couples, including many cases we have handled, where the wife makes the money and the husband has the bulk of child-care responsibilities.

Maybe It's Over . . . Where Do I Go From Here?

Mary Ellen sat down across the desk, forcing a smile. It was obvious that she felt uneasy visiting an attorney—not unlike many of the clients we have seen in our office over the past several years. After sixteen years her marriage was not what she and her husband wanted it to be, yet she was not sure a divorce was what she wanted either. We have to be candid with our clients: we're lawyers, not marriage counselors. We can advise prospective clients about the *legal* aspects of divorce, but we cannot advise them whether or not they *should* dissolve their marriage. When a client is uncertain or fearful, clarification of the legal and psychological issues involved frequently can help them to make the dissolution decision.

Mary Ellen needed to know about emotional and legal consequences of a divorce action and had taken the giant first step of coming to a lawyer. She didn't need to feel alone. In 1990, there were about 1,200,000 marital dissolutions granted in the United States.

I'm not here because of wife beating or alcoholism. Basically Jim and I just grew apart. Everyone thinks we're the all-American family. Justin is fourteen and Kristin's eleven. Jim and I are proud of our family.

We're also proud of what we've achieved. I don't really know where to start. We've worked so hard and it just now appears to be paying off. Jim has really accomplished a lot; I was alongside him every inch of the way. He has an MBA. I guess I feel it's my degree too, because I put him through school during the first years of our marriage. I taught high school English in Boston. We lived on my income. That made me feel important.

We came back to New York City fourteen years ago. Jim got the MBA, and I produced Justin. I haven't worked since then, at least not for pay. Oh, I've spent many, many hours working in the kids' schools and doing other volunteer work, but I haven't had a *real* job. I guess I believed my duty was to be a good wife and mother, so I never even updated my teaching credentials.

Anyhow, after we moved back home, Jim got a good job heading the marketing research department of a pharmaceutical firm. He stayed there for five years and then, nine years ago, he and two other fellows from the company started their own business. They formed a corporation that designs and produces medical supplies. Jim is responsible for the sales end of the operation. Now it's really starting to go, but I sure was frightened in the beginning. The loan we needed to start the business seemed overwhelming. For six months Jim did not draw a salary. We lived off our savings.

Actually, it really didn't take that long for the business to get off the ground. Six years ago we were able to buy our present home. Of course, we had the profit from the sale of our first home to help with the down payment, but at the time it seemed like a huge financial commitment.

So over the years we grew into a comfortable lifestyle, but when you strip away all our material possessions, there isn't much left. Of course we have the kids, but aside from them it gets awfully lonely in this marriage. Jim and I can barely agree on the time of day anymore. In fact, I'm just now recognizing all the subtle put-downs Jim has been handing me over these last years. Now I see how his put-downs have been eating away at my self-esteem, and the crazy part is that Jim still isn't even aware of what he has done. What I'm saying is that we aren't good for one another anymore.

What is right for us, all of us, including the children? Kristin needs braces—you know what that costs. Justin was just accepted into a very expensive private school. I want the kids to have all the advantages. What will a divorce do to their well-being?

Mary Ellen continued with some specific questions:

The kids are used to our home. Do you think I could keep it? Even if I can keep it, how can I afford to live there, or anywhere else for that matter? I haven't worked for so long; I really don't know that I could get a job. Besides, women just don't seem to earn that much money.

If we both want a divorce, does that mean that I'm entitled to "alimony"? How about the kids? Who'll pay for Kristin's braces and Justin's schooling, not to mention college, clothes, doctor bills, soccer shoes?

If Jim moves out, what will I do for money? What if he won't leave? Am I forced to move out? Will we end up hating each other? Does every divorce have to be ugly?

How will our kids behave? Our divorced friends' kids turn into monsters, especially when they bring home new "friends." I'm just assuming I would have custody of the children. Doesn't the mother always get custody?

How do you start a divorce? Can Jim and I both use the same lawyer? How long does it take? It seems as though all our friends' divorces dragged on forever.

I guess I'm just overwhelmed. Jim and I are unhappy in our marriage, but neither of us is sure that divorce wouldn't make a worse mess of our lives.

There aren't yes and no answers to all of Mary Ellen's questions. Speaking generally, one could say "Yes, you may get the house; yes, you probably will need to become employed; and yes, we'll make provisions for the children in the settlement agreement." But each divorce situation is unique, and a court or negotiating attorneys must consider many factors, including the age, income, and future earning capacity of the spouses. In settling the financial terms of divorce, every asset and liability of the parties has to be looked at. Few divorcing spouses will maintain their current standard of living with two households to support and not necessarily more income.

What will Mary Ellen do for money if Jim moves out? The courts make provisions for this. You will find an explanation of "temporary relief" in chapter eight, "Spousal Maintenance." In fact, as this book progresses it is our intention to answer all of Mary Ellen's questions and also the questions Jim has asked his attorney.

In answer to the question about both spouses employing the same attorney, in general an attorney should not represent clients on both sides of a conflict, since practically every marital dissolution involves conflicting interests between husband and wife. New York State's highest court, however, has ruled that an agreement that divided the spouses' property and settled custody and support would be enforced if its terms were fair, even though the attorney who drafted the agreement represented both husband and wife. A properly trained attorney can act as a mediator for both parties, and some attorney-mediators also draft the agreement that emerges from the mediation. If your agreement is drafted by someone who is not exclusively your attorney, we suggest that you have your own attorney review it before you sign.

Although men and women at the end of a traditional marriage face different factual problems, they often suffer from the same divorce-induced emotional problems. While our female clients may fear that they will not be able to survive economically, our male clients often fear losing their home, losing contact with their children, and losing many of their assets in a divorce court they suspect is biased in favor of women. Again, in some marriages the sex roles are reversed, or just different from the "traditional" marriage. Anger, guilt, hostility, anxiety, failure, rejection—these emotions don't favor men or women. Unwinding the legal relationship between spouses, although important, is usually only one act in a larger drama with many emotional aspects, which we have sketched in chapter two, "The Psychological Divorce."

Clients often need both legal and psychological advice. We regularly recommend counseling to clients who might benefit from it. Because Mary Ellen was not convinced that a divorce was the answer to her problems, that is what we did in her case. It is always wise to explore the alternatives before committing to divorce.

Most nonviolent couples should attend counseling sessions together because counseling involves three entities: the man, the woman, and the marriage. Patterns that are evident when couples attend together tend to be absent when they see the counselor separately. Couples who are able to go to counseling together are actually more likely to remain together. But even if these couples do dissolve their marriage, they often have an easier time of it because counseling teaches them to communicate better. If they are communicating, they can cooperate.

After three months of counseling, Mary Ellen scheduled an appointment to start the marital dissolution process. She had learned that she felt too much hurt and anger to stay successfully in the marriage. The counseling had helped clarify the problems; Mary Ellen was convinced now of the need to end her marriage.

Making the divorce decision did not prevent Mary Ellen from having strong and sometimes frightening feelings about the end of her marriage.

I feel guilty, and then I feel angry about the guilt, and angry at Jim because he never understood my needs. I know I want out, but still I feel a sense of failure. Why couldn't I make it work? Is it my fault? I thought my kids would be on my side, but they've really been very difficult. Justin is surly; he seems to always be angry with me. Kristin has become withdrawn and irresponsible.

Mary Ellen was clearly in the early stages of the psychological divorce process. She was startled but relieved to learn that she was fitting into a very normal pattern. We promised her that this phase would pass—and emphasized that right now we had work to do. Prior to this meeting we had sent her a large packet of preparatory materials that she was to complete and bring with her. She was to gather specific information regarding all of the tangible assets and liabilities accumulated during the marriage. We needed this in order to prepare what is known as a Verified Complaint for Divorce. We explained to Mary Ellen that a summons, usually together with a Verified Complaint, starts the divorce process in New York. The complaint includes provisions for child custody, visitation rights, support, and the division of property and debts.

Whatever your own situation, it will have similarities to the circumstances in Mary Ellen's case and certainly will have its own peculiarities. Divorce issues vary as much as people do. It is not practical to make an attempt to discuss them all. This book has been designed so that you can do much of the preparatory work yourself. As you work through each chapter you will gain knowledge and confidence. Reading of possible solutions to some of the legal and economic problems, you will begin to solve the psychological puzzles of your own particular situation.

For instance, chapter two, "The Psychological Divorce: Putting the Pieces Back Together," helps you understand your feelings and directs you toward creating a new life.

Chapter three, "Choosing Your Lawyer," is meant to help

you decide which lawyer out of the thousands available to you is the best for you in terms of ability, cost, and contribution to your personal comfort level. Chapter four, "Divorce Mediation: An Alternative," describes what we consider the most effective way for some couples to proceed with a divorce.

Chapter five, "Self-Help: Another Alternative," is both for those who want to do their divorce on their own without attorneys and for those who use attorneys but want to be better informed.

Chapter six, "The Basics of Negotiations," explores the attitudes you will need and suggests some of the tools that will make you effective in negotiating your own divorce settlement. Chapter seven, "Property Division," gives principles to use in solving the frequently difficult problem of splitting up what the couple owns.

Chapter eight, "Spousal Maintenance," deals with one of Mary Ellen's first concerns: how she will support herself and her children during divorce proceedings. Chapter nine, "Child Support," explains how parents' shares of support are calculated.

Chapter ten, "Child Custody," gives careful guidance toward finding the least harmful solutions. Chapter eleven, "Joint Custody," continues the discussion.

Chapter twelve, "Visitation," discusses possible ways to keep this aspect of divorce from breaking down into ugly confrontations.

Chapter thirteen, "Cohabitation and Alternative Lifestyles," is for those who choose not to (or cannot) be legally married. If you are one, you should be aware of the legal and economic consequences of your way of life.

The appendixes include a sample separation agreement, New York divorce statutes, and a historical and policy overview of New York divorce law by Professor Foster and Dr. Freed. Also included are the names and addresses of courts, agencies, and other services that can be called on for help through the rougher aspects of a divorce.

At the end of some chapters there are lists of additional questions. Use these lists—and this entire book—to help define and begin to solve all of the points that apply to your own divorce. But remember that while you will have learned more about the specific aspects of your divorce, no book can substitute for having a competent matrimonial attorney advise you.

CHAPTER TWO

THE PSYCHOLOGICAL DIVORCE: PUTTING THE PIECES BACK TOGETHER

THIS PSYCHOLOGICAL divorce chapter is different from the other chapters in the book which are about things like property division, child support, and cohabitation, which law school gives one tools to handle. Law school does not train one to be a psychologist. The 1987 edition of *Divorce in New York* recognized that fact by summarizing what the authors thought was the best of the mental health literature's concepts and generalizations about the psychological aspects of divorce.

Michael Stutman and I respect the generalizations that mental health professionals make about marriage and divorce, and we frequently use their materials in advising clients and often send clients to mental health professionals to get psychological support and perspective during the divorce process. But we limited this chapter instead to what I could say was true from my own experiences and left the rest to the mental health professionals. Appendix I lists books by mental health professionals that may help individuals in the various stages of the divorce process, and we recommend them.

One downside of this approach is that after twenty years of practicing family law, there are but a few things about the psychological aspects of marriage and divorce that I'm confident I know and yet are applicable generally to couples. Here they are:

WHAT MAKES A MARRIAGE SUCCESSFUL

FRIENDSHIP IS IMPORTANT

The best indicator of a good marriage is that the partners are best friends. I have seen such couples in real life, but nothing close has ever come through my office door as a divorce lawyer. My clients often say they respect their partner, or feel affection, loyalty, guilt, and a range of other emotions, but they almost never say they're good friends. Many, on the other hand, have come in and said they really don't like their spouse or enjoy being together. The realization that you and your spouse have not been good friends for a long time, if that is true, should make attempting the marriage's end easier. Maybe you are not losing so much after all.

SEX IS IMPORTANT

Clients often report that sex in the marriage died a year ago, two years ago, four years ago, even though the parties have continued to live together. One year I had several female clients, each of whom complained that her husband had lost interest in sex shortly after marrying, even though the sexual relationship had been fine before and for the first few months or years after the wedding. The couples were mostly in their forties, with no physical problems that would explain lack of interest and no suspected sexual involvements by the men outside the marriage. Feeling that an important part of her emotional life was missing, each of the women insisted that her marriage end, even though each husband wanted the marriage to continue.

The sexually uninterested spouse is sometimes the woman. Men have told me that the sexual relationship ended years before, when their wives suggested that their husbands sleep in another room because their snoring bothered them or some such reason. The wife then rejects the husband's sexual requests for one or another plausible reason, and the discouraged husband makes the request less and less frequently.

The parties continue sharing the same house for months or years before either does anything to end the legal marriage. I once told a husband that he had been committing emotional suicide by staying in such a relationship.

In any event, when a new client reports that sex in the marriage stopped or became very infrequent years ago, my experience tells me that the marriage is over and counseling is not going to save the relationship. But when sex is alive, even though there are lots of problems, I strongly recommend that the couple can see an appropriate counselor together and try to work things out.

Here again, the fact that a significant part of a healthy marriage has been missing should make accepting divorce easier for both spouses.

MANY PEOPLE STAY TOO LONG IN BAD MARRIAGES

Despite the repeats, I continue to be amazed at the answers to my question about when the marriage went bad. The couple has been married for twenty-odd years, and my client tells me that he or she has been unhappy in the relationship since the first year. The reasons for staying married vary, and I think much boils down to embarrassment and fear. There is a joke about a couple in their nineties appearing in court for a divorce. They tell the judge they've been married for seventy-five years and have been unhappy with each other from year one. The judge asks why they're getting divorced at such an advanced age. "Judge, we were waiting for the children to die."

I believe that people should work hard to make their marriages mutually satisfying, that we should do the nice things that *Reader's Digest*, women's magazines, and the professional literature say are needed to make a relationship grow. But I see in my practice so many years spent in relationships that were, at least in retrospect, failures almost from the beginning. Many of my clients who have endured poor marriages experience surges of joy, along with the usual depression, anger, and fear, when the divorce is at last done.

One lawyer's experience does not mean that marriages that have been bad for years do not get saved and become vibrant, satisfying relationships. Mental health professionals report such successful outcomes when the underlying psychological issues that prevent one or both spouses from having a good marriage are treated in therapy. As it happens, I have never seen them in my law practice.

DIVORCE IS ALMOST ALWAYS EMOTIONALLY DIFFICULT

Even if a marriage is very poor, it gives a certain structure to life that is upset by divorce. The stress varies, depending on many factors, including whether you are the one making the call that the marriage is over. In my experience, about two out of three marriages that end do so after the wife first makes that decision. Often she has thought about divorce for a year or two before taking a firm position, and the prospect of divorce is a shock to the husband, who has ignored the many signals of discontent his wife gave during that year or two. The initiating spouse may predominantly experience guilt, the other may be shaken to the core by the rejection, and both may be depressed, angry, afraid, and so forth. As in life itself, everyone has some pain during the exiting process.

IT IS UNWISE TO USE DIVORCE LITIGATION TO VENT NEGATIVE EMOTIONS

My six years of divorce lawyering since the original *Divorce in New York* have confirmed the book's premise that it is usually unwise, destructive, and self-destructive to use divorce legal procedures as weapons to punish one's spouse for his or her failings. There are lawyers who disagree. I had a discussion with a partner in a large New York City law firm shortly after the 1987 book came out who criticized the book's thrust, arguing that divorcing couples needed the "catharsis" of adversary litigation to really get over their marriages.

My experience is that everyone, including the couple's children, is better off if the divorce is completed without going to court except to get an uncontested divorce after a separation agreement is signed. In my practice the parties and the attorneys are almost always able to reach satisfactory agreements on the custody, support, and property division issues that should be settled before there is a divorce. When I do go to trial, which is only once or twice a year, it usually is because there is a fundamental, good faith difference of opinion and interests that cannot be compromised, such as whether the parties' children should live primarily with one parent on the East Coast or the other parent on the West Coast.

There are, of course, cases where one or the other spouse is so entangled with negative emotions that he or she cannot reach a reasonable settlement, one that would allow the parties and their children to get on with their lives with a minimum of handicaps. I try to let some time pass in hopes that the anger, hurt, or whatever will dissipate and allow a fair settlement. But if those emotions remain dominant, the legal force embodied in the New York Supreme Court is available to impose a solution to the couple's custody, support, and property issues. That has a price for each spouse in money, stress, lost time, and possible emotional damage to themselves and their children.

THERE ARE LOTS OF CHANGES AT A MARRIAGE'S END

The psychological reality of ending a marital relationship is complicated by the fact that numerous concrete problems, many of which seem overwhelming, often arise. Money that previously was devoted to maintaining one household will now have to be split between two. One or both of the parties may have to abruptly alter their standard of living or adjust their living patterns in order to meet their expenses. Disputes concerning the allocation of limited funds are likely to arise.

Separation and divorce usually require an adjustment in social relationship as the breakup sends a shock wave through the couple's network of family and friends. Although friends and family will offer comfort and support, the parties may have to recognize that their new single status distances them from this social circle. It is important to remind yourself that adjusting your life simultaneously to familial, financial, and social change requires a lot of energy, and you should pat yourself on the back occasionally simply for being able to deal with these changes.

If you seek the advice of an attorney you have entered the unfamiliar world of lawyers and the law. People turn to lawyers because they feel they need an expert who can protect their interests, who knows legal rules and procedures, and who can draft an enforceable settlement agreement and the other papers necessary for divorce. Depending on the lawyer you choose, you may feel even less control over the course of events than you did before. Not all lawyers are the same, and your choice of one, as discussed in chapter three, is very important.

YOU OWE YOUR KIDS A LOT

Parents will need to deal with their children and often to reestablish relationships with them. This will be a difficult hurdle for you to face and may produce the most guilt. Children seek explanations of what went wrong, and you, often unsure yourself about the answers, will have difficulty providing sufficient answers for them. Children often feel alienated and confused during and after a divorce, and it is crucial that both parents reassure them that they love them and will stand by them. Keep in mind that love and security in childhood are the building blocks to healthy, happy individuals and are the best gifts you can give your children.

Both parents should maintain an active, ongoing relationship with their children and should encourage each other to spend time with the children. When negotiating the specifics to accomplish this, the children's best interests should be paramount. The children should not be used as a bargaining tool to manipulate your ex-spouse into accepting your financial terms on a settlement. While this warning may seem self-evident, in the midst of the myriad shocks of divorce, even the best of parents can lose sight of their children's pain and confusion.

MENTAL HEALTH BASICS FOR DEALING WITH DIVORCE

The following are some basic principles on which most mental health professionals dealing with divorce—and we—agree.

YOU'RE NO ANGEL, BUT YOU'RE NOT SO BAD, EITHER

Altering your family status can be a serious threat to your perception of who you are in the world. Many spouses define themselves by their marriage and thus are devastated by the prospect of divorce: "If my marriage is a failure, then so am I." Besides seeing yourself generally as a failure, often you may see vividly where your spouse is at fault in the breakup of your relationship. Many people who are going through this process, whether they initiated the divorce or not, tend to see themselves as victims. It is important to remember that a relationship is a two-way street, and just as both parties contribute to the success of a relationship, so do both parties contribute, to a greater or lesser degree, to its failure. You should consider trying to change your frame of mind by seeing a counselor and reading self-help books. These sources can help you to deal with the negative emotions you are feeling, build a positive outlook, and boost your self-esteem so that you no longer see yourself as a victim.

ACCEPT THE PAST, DEAL WITH IT, AND GET ON WITH YOUR LIFE

The changes you are facing unleash an overwhelming, and at times a seemingly endless, stream of emotions. Amid the feelings of anger, fear, betrayal, failure, and disillusionment is the terrible feeling that what is happening is happening to you *alone*. It takes most people several months or years to come to terms with these feelings, but the process is worth the struggle.

Often the first stage that divorced couples experience, particularly the party who did not want the divorce and has not prepared himself or herself for it, is shock and denial. You may question whether the time you spent married was wasted. However, you must realize that you cannot completely obliterate the past or cut it out of your life. In order to deal with your past you must salvage something positive from it and integrate it into your new life.

This process of self-discovery will not be easy. It requires letting go of the feelings of hurt and anger that you have been clinging to and coming to terms with the reality of your marriage. It is crucial that you do not let these destructive feelings control you, as they will create a whirlpool effect, leading you deeper and deeper into depression. Letting go of these very painful and destructive feelings can be accomplished by accepting the reality of your past, learning something from it, and bringing those lessons with you as you build a healthier and more confident image of yourself. You must redirect your emotional investments from maintaining the relationship to maintaining yourself. When you finally do let go, you may have the urge to act on your emotional freedom. Some clients report scouring the entire house to purge it of anything that reminds them of their ex-partner. Others completely rearrange the furniture.

In the process of looking back you will learn how to look forward and move on with your life. This can be a very exciting stage. After coming through it most people arrive at a point where they can feel good about themselves, their bodies, and their capacities as creative and autonomous adults to deal with whatever life throws their way.

One danger is letting resentment toward your former spouse take too much of your energies. One psychologist I know, Pat Otis, warns against carrying "so much hatred that, like acid, it eats holes in your capacity to love."

HELP IS JUST AROUND THE CORNER

As mentioned above, one of the most painful feelings you are experiencing probably is the loneliness that results from separation or divorce. You need to learn to grow through loneliness to the state of aloneness, in which you are comfortable doing things by yourself and for yourself. This process often begins with a "hiding in the sand" period during which you may dive into your apartment or your work for weeks at a time. Each is an equally effective avoidance that is healthy over a short term, but it is dangerous over a long term.

One option that many people use to deal with the feeling of loneliness is joining a support group of similarly situated people. These groups can be very helpful, not only in helping people better understand the feelings they are experiencing but also in helping them counteract their natural tendency to feel that they are all alone.

Whether you choose to join an organized support group, or individual therapy, do further reading, or rely on your own network of family and friends, the best advice you can receive is to accept your situation, deal with your feelings, and build a stronger you. If your support group tends to place blame on the other party or encourage your self-pity, do yourself a favor and find another group. Their advice, while it may be tempting to accept, will retard your progress and will not help you move on with your life.

YOU SHOULD LOVE YOURSELF

Some divorced people find it easy to love others and quite difficult to love themselves. They are basically "half-people" attempting to find wholeness through loving another. A love based on a fear-filled flight from emptiness and loneliness is unlikely to last. Realizing your self-love is basic to all productive, vital, growing relationships. Self-love means that you accept yourself for who you are. We must each appreciate and understand our strengths and our weaknesses.

Self-love does not mean that you love *only* yourself, but rather that your capacity to love and accept others is founded on your love and acceptance of yourself. After a divorce it's typical to feel that you have no capacity to love either yourself or others. This is a self-esteem issue, and there are many exercises to improve the situation. For example, you could list five adjectives that describe yourself and then put a plus sign after each word that you think is positive and a minus sign after each negative. After you have done this, look at the negative adjectives and see if you can find anything positive about that particular aspect of your personality. The harder you work at this, the more positive things you're likely to find. Those who received scant love as children often have a great deal of difficulty loving themselves as adults. For some people, turning to (or returning to) their church or a particular clergyperson can be supportive and strengthening in this period.

Self-love is a particularly important issue for children involved in divorce. Many children feel that they have been shown to be unlovable, since one of their parents has left the home. They fear that the remaining parent will leave as well. This is a critical time for parents to do their best to reassure their children that they are cared for and deeply loved. This is very difficult for parents because children are often in need of the greatest love when their parents are least capable of providing it. Parents should make special efforts to explain to their children that even though they are having doubts about themselves and each other as a couple, they have no doubts about the love they feel for their children.

Those who have passed through the self-love trial often report that they emerge feeling securely lovable and that they no longer are afraid of being loved or of loving another.

START WITH FRIENDS, NOT LOVERS

Some recently divorced people complain that members of the opposite sex simply cannot be trusted. Trusting again is a difficult task for some, and it must be accomplished cautiously. The key to this stage is to *make friends, not lovers.*

Too often a divorced person plunges into a new romance too early, and the result is a relationship that is either dominating or desperate and often smothering. We must learn to trust before we can love safely.

Our incapacity to trust may be related to the wounds created by our divorce, or it may stem from childhood experiences. Some who have been deeply wounded find themselves either avoiding relationships or indulging in brief, exploitative relationships where the other party has little or no power. Others feel that they must make every relationship into a lifelong love relationship. Trying to *make* a lifelong relationship often does nothing more than prolong the adjustment process.

Trust is a two-way street: trust in yourself allows trust in others. Trust demands openness and openness exposes you to the risk of disappointment or rejection. Start slowly and cautiously. Using caution you can develop a healthier relationship style founded on your new sense of self-esteem. Clearly the rewards are worth the risks.

Trust is an issue for the children of divorce. As we have emphasized, children often will blame themselves for one parent's leaving unless the reason for the departure is clearly explained to them. The more trust you place in your children now, the more trust they are likely to place in you in the future.

SEX IS STILL IMPORTANT

Recently divorced people can be traumatized by the thought of dating. They feel they are old, unattractive, awkward, and no longer know the rules. Worse, they often have their parents' morality holding them back with the admonition to be "good." Furthermore, their own teenagers may be dictating their dating behavior by less-than-subtle suggestions. No wonder dating is confusing and uncertain and sexual hangups are so common.

Sexuality can be a major problem because it has been made such a big issue in Western culture. It is difficult to have a "normal" sexual relationship in a society where sex is used to sell everything from toothpaste to toenail clippers. Then, too, there is considerable confusion as to the role each gender should play in this era of feminism. Can a man still pay the check without making the woman feel dependent? Can a woman call up a man and ask him out without seeming forward? These and many other questions make the resumption of sexual relationships both frightening and fascinating.

During the early stages of divorce recovery it is common for the divorced person to be totally uninterested in sex. Often this is followed by a period of deep longing for sexual contact that can be very difficult to deal with. Some cannot accept the idea of sex without marriage, while others are unable to accept their sexual feelings at all. One way to deal with this problem is to recognize that our bodies need to be touched and held and that sexual contact is not necessarily the whole or the only answer to this need. Affection shown by and to friends and children can be a warm and reassuring way to maintain human contact until life can broaden out once more.

But as more personal—and potentially sexual—possibilities come into view, the key is to be both honest and cautious. Do not go beyond your comfort range, but do feel free to admit discomfort to your new social contacts. The fact that there are no clear rules for courting today can be frustrating, but it also provides you with the opportunity to set your own rules and create the best possible intimate relationship.

The sexuality stage is important for children because they need adult role models of both sexes. Children often are confused, frustrated, or intimidated by a parent's involvement in a new love relationship. Your attention, along with thoughtful and affectionate communication, is critical at this point. You must make a clear, sincere effort to talk frankly about sex and relationships. Remember that your child's strong reaction may be less of a response to your new relationship than to the fact that the child is just beginning to struggle with the whole notion of his or her own sexuality and independence.

It is very important to deal thoroughly with the issues raised here before proceeding to the next stage. Some indications that you have passed this stage are: you are comfortable going out with potential love partners; you know and can explain your present moral attitudes and values; you feel capable of having a deep and meaningful sexual relationship; your sexual behavior is consistent with your morality; and you are behaving morally—the way you would like your children to behave.

FREEDOM

Freedom in this sense is simply the freedom to be the person you were meant to be. This does not mean that your life will be blissful or that you will not run into any more problem relationships. Instead it means that you have freed yourself from the expectations that have controlled you. The greatest enemies of divorce recovery are not the other spouse or the legal process; rather they are the enemies that we all carry within us—such enemies as guilt, self-doubt, inadequacy, and fear of future relationships. When you achieve freedom you no longer focus on the past. You are able to plan a future on your own terms and in your own direction, where you can express feelings of anger, grief, loneliness, rejection, and guilt while actively pursuing a happy and self-fulfilling life.

———— ✤ ————

CHAPTER THREE

CHOOSING YOUR LAWYER

THE DECISION TO divorce is usually painfully difficult. Once it is made you are faced with another decision: do you hire a lawyer or do you represent yourself? If you decide to use an attorney, how do you find a lawyer who is right for you? The choice of an attorney is necessarily intertwined with another judgment you must make: do you want to try for a mediated or negotiated settlement without going to court? If you believe that you and your spouse are capable of negotiating a settlement either directly between yourselves or through your attorneys, then your attorney should have negotiating skills and the knowledge of New York divorce law and applicable tax law needed to draft a technically good separation agreement. The lawyer's litigation experience and ability are less important. However, if you believe that a war will be necessary to get satisfactory results with your spouse, or if your spouse has already hired a bomber as his or her attorney, then you may need a good courtroom lawyer to protect your interests effectively.

A PERSONAL DECISION

Before you select a lawyer you must assess your expectations of the attorney-client relationship. After all, you are buying into a highly personal, although temporary, partnership where mutual confidence is a key consideration. This relationship is highly individualized, so it is worth looking around before deciding on the attorney you will hire. Some lawyers can at once make a client feel secure and comfortable. Others may not be as personable but may be extremely imaginative in looking for solutions to your particular problems.

Do you expect the attorney to help you decide whether to divorce, or to act as a marriage counselor? If so, you probably are making a mistake. Most lawyers are not qualified to aid you in this way, unless they also are trained as marital therapists. Lawyers tend to be concerned primarily with getting the legal process started, documenting your financial situation, readying forms for filing, and developing effective strategies. These are the tasks they have been trained to do.

You also may wish to consider mediation (described in chapter four), and you may want to defer starting the formal legal process while you try mediation. You will need an attorney who is available for legal advice while you are in the mediation process and who can draft or review a technically sound separation agreement after you and your spouse settle the basic property, support, and custody issues in mediation.

Look for a lawyer whose practice is involved principally with marital dissolution work. A lawyer's fine reputation in immigration law, for example, is largely irrelevant to your needs. Ask if your potential attorney has been an active member of family law committees in local, state, or national bar associations or is a member of the American Academy of Matrimonial Lawyers, a group that admits only attorneys primarily doing family law. Also make certain your divorce lawyer has experience with the courts and the legal community of your area. But your own gut reaction, after you have gathered the necessary facts about the lawyer, is your most important guide in finding the right attorney for you.

THE ADVERSARY SYSTEM

This discussion of choosing an attorney, whose training and experience typically include both adversary negotiations and court trials, seems the right place to summarize our misgivings about divorce litigation. You may wish to raise these questions with your own prospective attorney and get his or her views on the costs and advantages of various approaches to ending your marriage.

This book leans against full-scale litigation and courtroom trials as a way of settling matrimonial disputes. Divorce proceedings with two hard-nosed attorneys facing each other in court or in no-holds-barred negotiating sessions may solve the legal and economic aspects of divorce while harming the social and psychological aspects, which are just as important. Dr. Max Cohen, a psychiatrist who does divorce mediation in New York, says the adversary system in divorce is perfect for very sick people. The litigation process encourages each divorcing spouse to use tools that will inflict severe pain on the other spouse, destroy whatever trust and goodwill are left in their relationship, and invite equal or greater pain as the other spouse retaliates.

The adversary process itself may leave each spouse embittered, even if a full-scale trial never occurs; preparing for a fault divorce trial is traumatic, as each spouse dredges up and relives those of the other party's bad acts that are relevant to trial. One woman we know described the effects of preparing for trial against her husband as "ripples." She said that five years after her case had been settled, on the eve of trial, those ripples were still doing damage, not only to herself and to her children but also to her friends and to her work. Such ripples from bitter divorces have contributed to adjustment problems in children, which show themselves in school performance, drug use, early pregnancies, and other problems. Prolonged stress from the process can even harm the divorcing spouse's physical health.

A real cost of litigation is that divorce terms that are imposed by a court are less likely to be complied with than settlements to which both parties agree. A judge can issue a piece of paper called a divorce judgment which imposes rights and obligations on the divorcing spouses, but the judge is not there to implement the orders. An aggrieved ex-wife or ex-husband can keep running back to court for orders enforcing the divorce judgment, but the process is expensive and in many ways unsatisfying.

PROBLEMS WITH DIVORCE LAWYERING

A very fine judge was recently the third speaker at a seminar for lawyers about the New York divorce law. The first two speakers had described with skill and clarity the complex, formal procedures the divorce lawyer can use to identify and to value a couple's marital property. The judge began, "When I hear the previous speakers say it takes two years to get a divorce case ready for trial, I say what about the clients?" He continued that a system that accepted leaving people in limbo for two years, neither really married nor divorced, might need to be replaced.

The lawyer is trained as an advocate. The adversary system of justice encourages and even demands that the attorney use every legal means available to gain an edge for his or her client. The essential problem—legally ending a dead marriage quickly, efficiently, and fairly with minimum damage to the spouses and to their children—often is forgotten as the spouses fight and watch their lawyers fight.

YOUR ATTORNEY FEES

Legal fees can be a problem in litigation or extended negotiations. Even with the best and most ethical attorney representing you, divorce litigation is expensive. It is time-consuming, and the lawyer is selling you his or her time. And, to be blunt, there are New York divorce attorneys who will intentionally make your divorce litigation longer and more complicated in order to increase their own fees. One judge who had sat for a year exclusively in the matrimonial part in New York County spoke of his experience there with an attorney who had been hired to represent the wife in a "large asset" case after another attorney had represented her in two years of negotiations and litigation. At a conference in court the judge thought that all the roadblocks to a settlement had been removed. The new attorney, however, said, "Judge, the case isn't ready to settle." The judge reviewed the issues that were solved and his view that the case was already settled. The new attorney had to repeat twice more "Judge, the case isn't ready to settle" before the judge understood that the attorney was not willing to let the case settle because he had not had enough time to build up legal fees.

Anger at an attorney and at legal fees is often, however, a client's way of venting anger at the fact of a divorce he or she does not want or at other history not related to the lawyer. The client may lack the courage or self-awareness to take responsibility for the marriage's failure and be tempted to make the lawyer, as a participant in an unwelcome process, the whipping boy.

Louise Raggio (Grier Raggio's mother and a Dallas attorney who has been helping people through divorces for forty years) once represented a female client of unusual self-insight and candor on this matter. The divorce had been concluded on favorable terms for the woman, yet she objected to paying reasonable legal fees and was extremely upset. In conversation she told Louise, "It hurts too much to be angry at my former husband and my children, and I have to blame someone, so I am taking my anger out on you."

Whatever your legal fees, we will give you odds that the money you pay your lawyer will not be the greatest cost of full-out adversary litigation. To avoid a matrimonial war it may be helpful to come from the point of view that you, as well as your spouse, are responsible for the breakdown of the marriage. If you are able to see yourself as responsible, you are well on your way to avoiding the "prove I'm right, prove he/she is wrong" scenario characteristic of litigation. Ideally both spouses and their attorneys will see the death of the marriage as creating a set of financial, legal, psychological, and social problems that they will work together to solve. In doing so they will create an appropriate post-marriage relationship that will support the couple's needs and the needs of their children.

REPUTATION AND RECOMMENDATIONS: KEY QUESTIONS

Most people choose lawyers through their reputations or by asking for recommendations from persons whose opinions they value. Divorced friends are a good source of information, particularly if their cases were resolved satisfactorily. Use caution, however, and evaluate your friend's lavish praise (or angry denunciation, for that matter). Inquire closely about those qualities that your friend either admired or disliked in the attorney. You may want to ask some of the following questions:

- Did the attorney's efforts interfere with or facilitate your friend's relationship with the former spouse and their children?
- Did your friend feel personally secure and comfortable with the attorney?
- Did your friend come away from the process feeling informed?
- Did your friend feel that the attorney's fees and the results of the divorce trial or settlement were fair?

If you follow this route, be sure to see the lawyer to whom you were referred, not his or her associate or partner. Remember that you may want to interview several lawyers before deciding on one who suits you. This is your right. You are the employer, and in such a critical matter as divorce it is essential that you find an attorney with whom you can communicate and in whom you can place your trust.

For personal referrals you also may turn to various organizations, your employer, or your labor union. In New York City the Association of the Bar of the City of New York at 36 West Forty-fourth Street, (212) 382-6625, will, through its Legal Referral Service, refer you to a lawyer selected as suited for your case. The initial consultation is usually around seventy-five dollars. Many other counties have Lawyer Referral Services; their addresses and phone numbers are listed in Appendix F. The New York State Bar Association has a state-wide Lawyer Referral Service in Albany, which New York residents may reach through an in-state toll-free number: 800-342-3661. Under their LRS plan a lawyer will consult with you for half an hour without charge or for a prescribed low fee, usually twenty-five dollars in cities. The LRS fee is fifteen dollars for the first half-hour in thirty-seven more rural counties. If your income is low you may qualify for free legal services through a legal aid program.

If you are referred to a lawyer who is a stranger to you, you can sometimes get background information about the lawyer by consulting the *Martindale-Hubbell Law Directory* in the public library. This directory includes a roster of most members of the bar in the United States and Canada and some other foreign countries. Listings paid for by the lawyer or the lawyer's firm appear in the directory's biographical section and include the lawyer's biography and educational background. The biographical listing frequently includes those areas of practice that the lawyer or firm emphasizes.

Legal Clinics: The Pros and the Cons

An alternate method of employing a lawyer may be to take advantage of one of the "legal clinics" that have appeared recently around the country and in your local Yellow Pages.

These clinics often handle uncontested divorces at low rates. They are able to charge less because they work on a large volume basis and use simple, standardized forms with extensive help from paralegal assistants. The clinic uses a factory approach, which is fine if only a small amount of property has accumulated during your marriage and there are no serious support or custody issues. Depending on where you live, an uncontested divorce might cost anywhere from $99 to $750, not counting filing fees. Fees charged by legal clinics usually are set in advance and are based on a published schedule. Lawyers are available during the day, in the evening, and on Saturdays; also, credit cards are accepted and the initial consultation is often free.

Remember that not all divorce cases lend themselves to the clinic approach; standardized procedures will not work for complex cases. A law clinic is simply a high-volume, high-efficiency law firm. Since the cost per case is low, the firm can afford to set low fees. High volume, however, carries its own risks. There probably will not be the expertise needed for complex cases. Clinics are rarely appropriate for cases that involve problems with property division or child custody.

THE INITIAL CONFERENCE: A CHECKLIST

During the initial conference you should ask the lawyer questions as well as give information. You need information to determine whether this attorney should handle your case. Your basic standard for choosing will be your own gut reaction to the lawyer personally and as a professional, but answers to the following questions may assist you in formulating or reinforcing that reaction.

1. What are his or her credentials?

   a. Having attended a well-known law school is no guarantee of outstanding ability; however, it helps to know the lawyer's academic background.

b. Does the lawyer belong to the city or county bar association? This may indicate respect among peers and suggest respect among the local judges.

c. You can check to see on which sections or committees of the bar association the lawyer has served. If he or she has served on sections or committees related to family law, such as the family law section or the taxation section, or if the lawyer is a member of the American Academy of Matrimonial Lawyers, chances are you're dealing with one of the more committed lawyers in your area.

d. Look around the office—you'll see the degrees, diplomas, professional memberships, and honors the lawyer has attained. Perhaps you will not even need to ask about credentials.

2. What portion of the lawyer's time is spent in family law matters? Many lawyers, particularly in New York City, now deal almost exclusively in divorce cases.
3. Is the lawyer willing to discuss the attitudes of local judges concerning issues relevant to your case? Many lawyers are able to predict accurately in most cases what the general outcome of a trial would be, based on the prevailing judicial attitudes. Getting the client to accept those predictions is often the hardest part of our job. This would be a good time to discuss specific strategies for your case.

YOU ARE THE EMPLOYER: A CLIENT'S BILL OF RIGHTS

It is important to let your lawyer know exactly what quality and type of legal service you expect. According to some studies, there are enormous differences between the client's view of what was wanted from legal services and the lawyer's view of what the client wanted.

Although lawyers often assume that the result is the main criterion used by clients in evaluating their services, other less tangible factors are often more important to the client. One survey concludes that clients respond more favorably to friendliness, promptness, and lack of condescension and value being kept informed by their lawyers.

You can control your own divorce proceedings by paying attention to the following, which we call the Client's Bill of Rights (and responsibilities):

1. Find out your lawyer's qualifications and experience in family law matters at the first consultation.
2. Insist on a written retainer agreement that explicitly sets out the lawyer's responsibilities and fee structure.
3. Stay informed about the progress of your case by requesting copies of all letters and documents prepared or received in the lawyer's office in your behalf. Ask questions—communication is a two-way street.
4. Determine early how the lawyer plans to represent you and what course of action is expected to be taken during the divorce process.
5. Be aware that you can always change lawyers, even if you have signed an agreement. As long as you have paid to the point at which you part, the lawyer cannot prevent you from taking your file with you should you decide to change lawyers.

Again, the relationship between client and lawyer is that of employer and employee. You are the employer, and you have an absolute right to fire your employee at any time, even without cause. Note, however, that when you change lawyers you will duplicate some of your expenses up to that date because your new attorney will have to become familiar with the facts of your case, and you will likely to have to pay for the time this will take.

Conversely, there are a number of responsibilities that you as a client should observe and certain realities you must recognize if the lawyer is to be as effective and as efficient an advocate as he or she can be:

1. Your lawyer cannot guarantee results. Although the lawyer can, and probably will, make predictions about the outcome of your case, the actual outcome of negotiations or litigation may turn on very complex factors.
2. Always keep your lawyer informed of any new developments that might affect your cause.
3. Take your lawyer's advice, or get another lawyer. You are wasting your money and the lawyer's time if you do not have confidence in the lawyer's special knowledge and skills.
4. Be utterly candid with your lawyer; tell the truth. Legal advice is worthless if based on faulty or partial information. Tell your lawyer every fact that is relevant to the situation, being careful to include all facts that do not appear to be in your favor. Lawyers can plan effective strategies around adverse facts, but only if they are aware of them.

THE ATTORNEY'S ETHICS

You should expect and demand from your lawyer nothing short of utmost zeal, confidence in you, and honesty. Once retained by you, the lawyer is obligated, both by law and by the lawyer's own ethical code, to be completely loyal to you. The lawyer should permit neither personal interests, interests of other clients, nor the wishes of third persons to diminish his or her total commitment to you. This includes a commitment to accept employment only for matters in which he or she is competent. If the lawyer does not have the expertise to handle your particular divorce case, he or she should refer you to an attorney who does.

If you become dissatisfied with your lawyer and decide to use another, you should be aware that New York permits the original lawyer to assert a lien against whatever paperwork you have already provided in connection with your case. If the papers are originals that you need for your divorce or other matters, the lawyer has great leverage against you until you have paid the fee. Your new lawyer can help you negotiate this matter.

If you believe that your lawyer has overcharged you, acted unethically, or failed to represent you fully, report this to the disciplinary committee or grievance committee responsible for the lawyers in your county. These committees operate under the supervision of our appellate judges for disciplining unethical lawyers. For more information contact the bar association in your county or speak to a clerk in your county's courthouse. Appendix G is a list of New York State's supreme courts by county, with addresses and phone numbers.

CHAPTER FOUR

DIVORCE MEDIATION: AN ALTERNATIVE

CONCEPTUALLY, DIVORCE mediation is the most civilized and efficient way for many couples to resolve their end-of-marriage disputes. When the mediation chapter for the 1987 edition of this book was written, it was anticipated that divorce mediation would take off in New York and become a very common way of reaching settlements. That hasn't happened as yet. On the political front, some representatives of women's groups have attacked mediation as a process in which the woman, often the more economically passive spouse, is short-changed at the marriage's end. The argument is that the dependent spouse needs an aggressive lawyer advocate to insure that she gets her reasonable share or, as it is sometimes put, as much as she can get.

We have never done divorce mediation in our practices, but have suggested to clients that they consider doing mediation with a competent professional. The acceptance rate for the suggestion has been very low. Also, we have had a few cases where the client wanted a divorce based on an agreement that had been reached after a lengthy mediation and which was later completely rejected by the other spouse after consultation with an attorney. This leaves a very angry client and a situation that is worse than if the mediation process had never occurred.

We still believe that mediation is the best way for some

couples, and respect many of the professionals who are doing mediation in New York. Lenard Marlow is a good friend who gave up a successful career doing divorce litigation in the early 1980s and, at substantial financial sacrifice, began doing divorce mediation. He has written several books on mediation and the divorce process, and many of his ideas are used in this chapter.

A BETTER IDEA?

Intense property, custody, and support disputes sometimes come from and express the former couple's underlying emotional conflicts. One premise of divorce mediation is that the anger, hurt, resentment, depression, and guilt a spouse carries from the marriage almost always needs to be addressed and handled carefully as part of a divorce. A second premise is that the adversary system, whether in court or in formal negotiations, may make a spouse feel less secure, more threatened, more depressed, and more hostile, both in itself and by encouraging aggressive expression of each person's negative feelings.

To some extent we separate the psychological divorce discussed in chapter two from the litigated or negotiated property, custody, and support terms of divorce, leaving the divorcing spouse's emotional needs to his or her therapist, friends, or other resources. The importance of mediation is that it is an alternative process, one in which the parties work together to resolve their emotional needs, during the same time that the financial and custody aspects of a divorce are decided. This chapter should help you decide whether divorce mediation might work for you.

Divorce mediation has come in for more attention nationally than it has in New York. California, for instance, has required mediation of child custody disputes since 1981, and mediation is more common in other western states as well.

Mediation puts the mediator in the middle, since mediators

deal with both spouses' needs and feelings as they assist them to negotiate and to settle their disputes. A skilled divorce mediator is usually a matrimonial attorney or a trained therapist. The mediator will meet with both parties together and will encourage them to see the issues in terms of joint problems to be solved rather than as conflicts. For instance, a skilled mediator is likely to phrase the custody question as "How can we insure that both of you will have the quality and amount of time with the children necessary for them to get full benefit from each of you as parents?" rather than as "Who gets custody of the kids?"

The competent mediator, working with both spouses together, will encourage each to express any basic emotional issues that are standing in the way of ending the marriage, if it must be ended, with minimum damage. For instance, the wife may say that she can't trust anything her husband says about his business. She may, in fact, believe that he would lie to defraud her of property; but perhaps what she really means is that she is so hurt by his betraying her and going off to live with another woman that she no longer feels that she can trust him about anything. In mediation she may be able to first express and then separate that pain from reasoned judgment; and, based on years of having shared everything with her husband regarding their finances, she may conclude that he very likely is telling the truth about money issues. Lenard Marlow says that in his experience with mediation problems "dissolve" as their emotional underpinnings are dealt with.

WHAT IS DIVORCE MEDIATION?

Divorce mediation seeks to resolve the same issues as are handled by negotiations between opposing attorneys or by a court trial. It just attempts to get them there by a different route. When you start adversarial divorce proceedings you are employing other people to do the job for you—lawyers to "negotiate" an agreement or, if they are unable to do that, a judge to "order" one. Divorce mediation, on the other hand, seeks to help you conclude an agreement yourselves. The hope is that since it will be your own agreement, it also will be one that you can live with.

Divorce mediation sees itself as being an empowering process. A divorce mediator believes that it is the two of you who are the experts and the ones best qualified to make important decisions in your lives. From the mediator's standpoint the problem is that you have lost the ability to do that. A divorce mediator's function, therefore, is to help restore that ability to you. Instead of disempowering the two of you by having you turn those decisions over to others, divorce mediation hopes to empower you to be able to make them yourselves. For that purpose it provides you with the assistance of a neutral third party, called a mediator, whose primary function is to be a facilitator of communication between the two of you. And it then provides you with the information and the setting that will enable you to use his or her assistance effectively.

In most instances the two of you would be unable to conclude an agreement on your own, for two reasons. First, you lack the information that is necessary for you to make the informed, intelligent decisions needed to properly conclude an agreement—not only the technical information about the law, but also the practical information about being divorced and the problems that you should anticipate in the future. Second, and perhaps most important, the circumstances that have brought the two of you to this point in your lives also have created an atmosphere filled with very painful feelings. These feelings would make it difficult, if not impossible, for the two of you to discuss the issues that you are confronted with, let alone to resolve them, on your own. That is why you need help.

Divorce mediation proceeds on the assumption that if you are given the right help in the right setting, you can overcome those obstacles and conclude an agreement on your own, without the intervention of lawyers and judges. The setting is the informal one provided by a mediator's office, rather than the more formal one provided by an attorney's conference room or by a judge's courtroom. The mediator, the mediator's "advisory attorney," and/or your own attorney will provide you with legal information and answer questions you may have as you go along. Help will come from the mediator, who will serve as the communication facilitator between the two of you. Divorce mediation rejects the idea that separating and divorcing couples are unable to communicate with each other. They communicate all the time. It is just not effective or productive communication. What they need is the assistance of a third person who will serve to open up the avenues of communication and, just as important, help to make that communication effective to produce an agreement between them.

Mediators believe that the mediator's office is best suited to open up the necessary channels of communication and that mediators can best help you to separate the practical problem of divorce from the feelings that are obstacles to resolution. A skilled mediator tries to provide you with the bridge that you need to overcome those feelings and conclude an agreement. If you are able to do that you will be left with your own agreement—one that you have concluded and have agreed to accept—rather than one that you may feel was imposed on you.

How Is It Different?

Mediation is often confused with conciliation and arbitration. There is considerable overlap in the techniques used for each process, but in general, proceeding from mediation to conciliation to arbitration involves giving an increasing amount of power to the neutral third party. Basic definitions are as follows:

> Mediation: the process of bringing in a neutral third party to help two disputing parties come to a mutually agreeable settlement. The mediator does no individual counseling. The mediation role is limited to (1) proposing basic ground

rules for the parties' sessions to "keep them on task," (2) helping the parties define or clarify the issues at hand, including emotional issues, and (3) exploring alternative solutions so spouses can come up with a settlement that best fits their particular interests and circumstances.

Conciliation: the traditional distinction between conciliation and mediation is that the conciliator takes a more active role than the mediator in resolving the conflict and in perhaps saving the marriage. Rather than simply being referees, conciliators may present their own solutions to a couple's problems. This distinction is sometimes blurred, however, because divorce mediators often use conciliation tactics in mediation.

Arbitration: again, a neutral third party is used here, but the spouses agree to give the arbitrator, such as a private judge, the power to *decide the dispute.* In fact, some arbitrators are retired judges, and both sides are often represented by lawyers. In *binding arbitration* the parties agree beforehand to abide by the decision of the arbitrator, as if it were law. The best source for traditional arbitrators is the American Arbitration Association, which is listed in your local phone directory.

Mediation is both a process and a product. As a process for parents it forges a transition for the couple from a love-parenting relationship to a parenting relationship. The product of mediation should be more than the terms of a divorce; there also should be a mutually acceptable working agreement between parents who have gained from the mediation process an enhanced capacity to settle future disputes on their own.

Mediation keeps the power with the divorcing individuals. It provides an opportunity to structure parent-child relationships, to decide property questions, and to set support on the participants' terms instead of the lawyers' and the courts' terms. The feelings and principles of the people involved will form the basis for any mediated settlement. According to the late O. J. Coogler, one of the founders of modern family mediation, the "basic rule of structured mediation is that there should be no victims."

Coogler also believed that the participation and fairness of mediation prevents parties from being victimized. At a minimum, fairness means that family assets must be fairly distributed according to the needs and contributions of all and that children must have access to both parents.

Naturally, each side's concept of fairness can change during mediation. According to John Haynes, a former associate of O. J. Coogler, "that's the magic of mediation." Mediation should hold a mirror up to each party so that he or she can better see the impact of his or her demands and better understand the needs of the other.

Mediators can help their clients deal with anger, fear, and other feelings so that these do not block the progress of settlement. Mediation demands that spouses communicate honestly with each other in a structured setting where they are encouraged to clearly state their principles and positions and to negotiate in good faith. This can be difficult at first. Some spouses are flatly unwilling to mediate or are incapable of doing so. An exercise to determine your willingness and capacity to mediate is presented later in this chapter.

MEDIATION—HOW IS IT DONE?

The actual techniques of mediation differ with each practitioner and family. According to John Haynes,

> One part of mediation is to lay out all the options. I look at every problem in divorce as a skein of wool that has to be carded. We have to look at each problem—children, finances, the family home—one by one. Then I will try to separate out each problem into component parts. Then I look at all the options I can think of and ask the parents to think of options of their own. . . . Perhaps it's the way we were educated, but most people come in with this idea that there is really just one way to do things; that there's just one way to think about dividing up the children's time, for instance, when there are perhaps five or six ways, or

more, and we can begin to explore all the options before making any decisions.

With rare exceptions, mediation of custody disputes is future oriented. The past cannot be changed. The task is to determine how, starting right now, the parties can become cooperative, responsible, and separate parents.

There are a number of mediation procedures. O. J. Coogler's "structured family mediation" uses one mediator, who is not an attorney, plus an advisory attorney who is brought in later in the process to answer deferred legal questions and draft the settlement agreement. Mediation by two mediators (one a family law attorney and the other a trained therapist) is also possible and may be more effective in dealing with difficult cases. Under Coogler's system mediation sessions take place once a week and last two hours each.

Coogler has prescribed six basic rules for mediation in *Structured Family Mediation Method*:

1. The mediator cares about both parties and their children but will not represent any side.
2. The participation of both parties in mediation is voluntary, but the mediator will not allow either side to coerce, abuse, or lay blame in an effort to force the other to agree to take any particular action.
3. Everything that occurs in mediation is confidential and should not be used in court if mediation does not succeed.
4. Any agreement the couple comes up with must be based upon adequate information, which means that both sides must agree to fully disclose what they know about family finances.
5. The mediator cannot require the mother and father to cooperate, but he or she can keep them from negotiating with one another in noncooperative ways. In other words, minimum civility is required during these sessions.

6. The mediator will not endorse any agreement regarding the custody of a child that does not provide for contact with both parents.

In Lenard Marlow's mediation structure a couple is assisted throughout mediation by an "advisory attorney," whose function is to answer whatever legal questions either spouse may have. Since that attorney does not represent either party individually, that information is given in a different spirit and for a different purpose than in a conventional attorney-client relationship. The advisory attorney will act as the dispenser of information, not as an advocate. In keeping with the spirit of mediation, the advisory attorney will never meet with either spouse individually, since he or she wants both spouses to hear the same information. The advisory attorney in Marlow's model has a second function as well, and that is to draft the agreement the couple ultimately will sign.

Divorce mediators following John Haynes's model, who are usually therapists, not attorneys, prepare a "memorandum of understanding." This is a summary of the agreement that the couple has concluded with the mediator's assistance. The mediator then will refer them to an attorney with whom he or she has worked in the past, who will prepare a formal separation agreement, or ask them to take the memorandum of understanding to their own separate attorneys to prepare the final document.

Marlow argues that it is unwise for the couple to take the divorce mediator's memorandum of understanding to their own separate lawyers. The result may be disputes between their attorneys about language or substance, and if the couple is not careful their agreement can come apart in the process. This is particularly so if the two parties do not go back to the mediator with their attorneys' concerns. The mediator, who had been successful in getting the spouses to an agreement, has been bypassed and the discussions between the two attorneys may simply become the adversarial process that the couple was attempting to avoid in the first place.

If the advisory attorney is an experienced lawyer, he or she should prepare a draft of the final agreement. Each spouse will still have the same opportunity to take it and review it with his or her separate counsel and to make whatever changes that may be necessary. If the spouses have a single document there will be less danger that their lawyers will argue over language, and the costs will be kept down.

PROBLEMS WITH MEDIATION

There are difficulties with mediation just as there are difficulties with what sometimes happens to divorcing couples who litigate. In particular, mediation is dangerous for a spouse who has been financially and emotionally subordinate during the marriage. Unless the mediator is very good, the agreement reached in mediation may be a continuation of the control or intimidation that the stronger spouse has exercised previously over the weaker. It is doubtful that mediation is ever appropriate where there has been a pattern of physical battering on the part of either spouse.

Mediation also requires the voluntary participation of both spouses, and in many cases only one party wants the divorce. In my experience it is wives who more often begin the legal divorce process, and they do so after a year or more of telling their husbands they want a divorce. The other spouse often is unwilling to participate in a mediation process leading to divorce, sometimes in hopes that the mediation request is just more divorce talk that will go away if ignored.

Mediation does not remove your need to be advised by a competent lawyer, and your counsel should serve as a check against your signing an unwise agreement. Your lawyer should tell you whether the financial, custody, and support deal you are negotiating with your spouse is more, less, or about equal to what a judge would do for you after a divorce trial. A good lawyer can help you guard against one danger of mediation—that the informal, out-of-court procedures will miss or improperly value property that should be divided between the spouses. Once the basic terms are settled, an attorney, probably the mediator's advisory attorney, should write them into a separation agreement.

SELECTING A MEDIATOR

Finding the right mediator is critical, for there are large differences in the quality of divorce mediators. Some are excellent; others are not. Here are some simple do's and don'ts that will help you. No one of these is an acid test, and you should give much weight to your own gut reactions.

1. What are the mediator's credentials in his or her profession of origin? The person who you will be considering has not gone to graduate school to obtain a degree in divorce mediation. It's a new field and no such degree is available. The mediator probably started out as either an attorney or a mental health professional. If the mediator is an attorney, did he or she specialize in matrimonial law or was he or she a corporate lawyer? Obviously a divorce lawyer will have had far more experience dealing with the problems with which separating and divorcing couples are confronted than will a corporate attorney. If the mediator is a mental health professional, was his or her primary experience working with couples in family therapy? Again, a mediator who has had extensive experience working with couples probably will do better as a divorce mediator than someone who has spent his or her professional life testing children in a school.

2. What standing does the divorce mediator have in his or her profession of origin? If the divorce mediator is an attorney and professes to have a background in family law, has he or she served on the matrimonial and family law committees of the state bar association? Is he or she a fellow of

the American Academy of Matrimonial Lawyers? If the mediator is a mental health professional, is he or she a member of the American Association of Marriage and Family Therapists? In either case, has the mediator written any books or articles on the subject or presented any lectures or workshops at any state or national divorce mediation conferences?

3. If the mediator is not an attorney, does he or she work with an attorney? The best mediator would have the technical knowledge of an experienced divorce lawyer and the human understanding and interpersonal skills of a good mental health professional. It is not surprising, therefore, that the best divorce mediators are those attorneys and mental health professionals who have learned from one another. If the mediator you are considering is an attorney, does he or she have the disposition and the personal outlook that you would expect of a mental health professional? If the mediator is a mental health professional, will you also be assisted in the process by an attorney who can provide you with the technical information you will need as you go along?

4. What is the mediator's reputation? If you are considering using a particular mediator, check him or her out. Most mental health professionals, attorneys, and even members of the clergy in your community know who are considered to be good in their community. Ask them whether they have heard of the mediator you are considering and what his or her reputation is. Better yet, ask a number of professionals for their recommendation. If you hear the name of a particular mediator over and over again, that should tell you something. By the same token, if you never hear the name of a mediator you are considering, that should tell you something also.

5. What materials will the mediator provide you to help you make informed, intelligent decisions? Divorce mediation is not supposed to be a once-over lightly. On the con-

trary, you have some very important decisions to make. To be sure, mediators proceed on the assumption that these are your decisions, not theirs. Nevertheless, that does not mean that you should be left in the dark or on your own. Thus, you will need not only the interpersonal skills that the mediator will bring to his or her work, but also the information necessary to enable you to make intelligent decisions.

6. Is divorce mediation the mediator's primary occupation? All things being equal, someone who spends all, or a majority, of his or her time as a divorce mediator would be expected to have more experience, and more expertise, than someone who simply practices divorce mediation on the side. By the same token, he or she would be expected to have a greater commitment to his or her work.

7. Is the mediator a professional, and do you feel comfortable with him or her? As a rule, people who strike you as being competent and intelligent will generally do competent, intelligent work. Even though you will be making the decisions in mediation, you are nevertheless reposing a lot of trust in the mediator you choose. It is therefore very important that you feel that he or she is a professional, takes his or her job seriously, and is genuinely concerned in helping you. Ideally you should feel that the mediator you choose has "balanced judgment," is understanding, and is genuinely concerned in helping you. If you are very lucky he or she may even possess some wisdom. The term for all of this is professionalism.

8. Shop around. While it may be difficult to judge a particular mediator, it is not that difficult to compare them. Most mediators do not charge for an intitial consultation, so it will cost you nothing to meet with them. It is not necessary to meet with a dozen mediators. Take the two people whose names you hear most often and make appointments with them. Then you will be able to decide.

In selecting a divorce mediator there are also certain things that you should not do.

1. **Don't emphasize price.** This is probably the most common, and the most fatal, mistake. Concluding an agreement through divorce mediation should save you a great deal of money, as the cost probably will be only a small fraction of what it would cost were the two of you to retain separate attorneys to negotiate that agreement for you. You need the very best mediator that you can find. All separation agreements are not the same. You may not know the subtleties, but that doesn't mean that they don't exist and need to be handled properly.

2. **Don't put too much stock in "diplomas"** that state that a mediator has completed a training course in divorce mediation or has been certified by a local or state organization. Someone who would like to stand out as a divorce mediator may obtain these "qualifications" because he or she lacks others. Worse yet, the organization that hands out the diploma or does the certification may be in the business of doing only that. In short, those pieces of paper are no substitute for the competence that you need.

CONCLUSION

By all means consider mediation. In fact, consider all of your options. You are at a difficult crossroads in your life. While there may be many people who will urge you to leap before you look, that is not wise counsel. Consult with a divorce lawyer. Meet with a mediator. (While you will consult with a divorce lawyer on your own, the mediator will meet with the two of you together.) Then decide where you feel most comfortable and which procedure you think is best for you. But make that decision only after you have done your homework. The decision you are making is an important one and therefore should be made carefully.

CHAPTER FIVE

SELF-HELP: ANOTHER ALTERNATIVE

IF YOU AND YOUR spouse are able to agree on the property division, maintenance, child custody, child support, and visitation issues that need to be settled, it is possible that you will be able to prepare the necessary papers in order to have a court enter a judgment that grants the divorce. We are, however, reminded of the adage "It is possible to build your own house—but most people hire contractors." The analogy to home building is appropriate for a complex divorce, as you will be living with its terms for years to come. But the reality is that many couples cannot afford to hire attorneys to help them. In New York County about half of each year's fifteen thousand divorces go to parties who are not represented by attorneys.

We have practiced in states other than New York and have spoken with attorneys across the country, and we believe that New York has some of the country's most complicated and arcane procedures for obtaining a divorce. Other states have done better. For instance, Arizona changed its Rules of Civil Procedure in 1991 to simplify its procedures and authorize "divorce-by-mail" so long as there are no minor children and no complicated financial issues. Another Arizona procedural innovation that self-represented litigants frequently use is the evening court, available two nights a week for those who are unable to attend court appearances during the day. A report prepared for the American Bar Association's Special Committee on the Delivery of Legal Services found that 88 percent of divorce cases filed in Arizona in 1990 involved at least one litigant who self-represented, and in 52 percent of the cases neither spouse had an attorney. Seventy-two percent of the self-represented petitioners were satisfied enough that they would select the same type of representation again.

Hopefully New York's complicated procedures will be changed by the time you read this book. New York State's former Chief Judge, Sol Wachtler, appointed a committee of judges and lawyers in September 1992 to review the conduct of matrimonial attorneys and the effectiveness and appropriateness of the existing adversarial system. The committee's goals, according to Chief Judge Wachtler, "are to improve access to the justice system and to improve the system's ability to provide a fair and effective tribunal for matrimonial actions." We suggest that you express support for what Chief Judge Wachtler was trying to do by telling your state legislator that changes should be made in New York's statutes and procedures to make them less technical and more user friendly.

But for now we deal with the system as it is. The procedure that follows assumes that a divorce will be obtained on the ground that you and your spouse entered into an agreement, lived apart for one year, and have honored the terms of the agreement. This is the closest thing that New York has to "no-fault" grounds for divorce; most other states grant true no-fault divorces based on either participant's telling the court that the marriage has ended. New York's "fault" grounds for divorce include: abandonment for one or more years, adultery, confinement in prison for more than three years, and cruel and inhuman treatment. A discussion concerning how to obtain a divorce under any of these grounds is beyond the scope of this book.

The first step toward obtaining a divorce on the grounds that you have lived separate and apart for one year or more pursuant to a written agreement is to prepare the written agreement, often titled a Separation Agreement. The separation agreement must include all of the terms that you have agreed to and must be signed by both you and your spouse in the same way as you would execute a deed. We have included a sample of a separation agreement as Appendix A. As you can see from the sample, the provisions of the separation agreement can be very detailed.

It would be hard to overstate the importance of the substance, and the form, of this document. We have been involved in cases, some with millions of dollars at stake, where the validity of the agreement (and therefore its effectiveness) was determined by the way the agreement was signed. The agreement must be "acknowledged" before a notary public; simple notarization of your and your spouse's signature is not enough.

The separation agreement will be used by you and your spouse to determine all of your rights and responsibilties concerning everything the two of you did while you were married. In the future various courts may be asked to interpret the agreement. These courts may, for example, look at the agreement from a tax or a bankruptcy standpoint. In many cases your agreement will be interpreted as though you had all of these consequences in mind at the time you made the agreement, even if ten or more years have gone by. If you have children the agreement may have an even longer effect.

After you have prepared the agreement you should each properly sign at least four complete copies, two for each of you. Although it is not required until you actually start the divorce proceedings a year later we recommend that you take one of your copies and file it with the county clerk's office in the county where you live. We recommend that you do it sooner rather than later because documents can be misplaced and the filing fees may increase.

When you file the agreement you will be given an "index number." This number is to your divorce what your social security number is to you; be sure to keep it handy. The addresses and telephone numbers of the county clerks are in

Appendix G. While the county clerk's office is not allowed to give you legal advice, it is a good source of knowledge about forms and procedures. One of the matrimonial clerks in New York County says they help people who are doing their own divorces in the same way that an auto parts sales-person helps someone who is building a car. The clerk can show you the forms you need but will not fill them out for you. We suggest that you call your county clerk before you make the trip. Find out what the filing fee is, what hours they are open, and what form of payment is required (generally, personal checks are not accepted).

Once a year has passed from the time you signed the agree-ment (not from the time you separated), and if you have honored your obligations in the agreement, you may start an action for divorce. If you haven't already done so, you must now file the separation agreement with your county clerk's office. Then you must prepare a fairly extensive number of documents.

The first is a summons. This form gives your spouse notice that divorce action has been commenced, the type of "relief" you are asking for, and the amount of time your spouse has to respond to your demands. As we are assuming that your spouse will not be contesting the divorce, no response from him or her will be necessary.

Next comes a verified complaint. This shows the court that you have met the New York residency requirements, the type of marriage ceremony that you had (civil or religious), that you have grounds for divorce, whether there are minor chil-dren of the marriage, and what relief you are requesting. You need to exercise care in preparing this document, as it tells the court what you are asking for. If you don't ask for it in your complaint, the court probably won't give it to you in the judgment. You must file the summons and complaint with the court clerk and buy an index number before the summons and complaint are served on your spouse.

From this point on, the types, numbers, and particular con-tents of the various documents that you are required to prepare are varied. You can get a sense of what is required by contacting your court clerk's office and going by a stationery store that carries legal forms. Some stores and divorce services have kits with instructions.

Once you have all of your papers together you will present them to the appropriate department in your county clerk's office, where they will be reviewed and, if acceptable and if the required fees have been paid, transmitted to a judge or referee for review. If your papers conform to the law's requirements the judge will sign the judgment of divorce. In some counties you give a postcard to the county clerk, who mails it to you when your papers have been signed and entered in the clerk's files. At that point you are divorced and you should serve a copy of the judgment on your spouse.

We have not mentioned what needs to be done in order to transfer assets that may have been divided in the separation agreement. For example, if a house is given to one spouse, or if a pension is to be divided, or if life insurance policies are being transferred, there are various forms, tax returns, and possibly court orders that may be necessary. These matters can be complicated and vary with each couple's situation.

DOING YOUR OWN LEGAL RESEARCH

If you do your own divorce, you may want to research statutes and cases. Even if you have an attorney handling your case, reading some court opinions in divorce cases and statutes will make you a more informed, and perhaps more powerful, client. But please do not assume that reading this book and a few cases makes you a matrimonial lawyer. The divorcing spouse with a complicated situation needs a professional in his or her corner. With that limitation in mind, let's look briefly at what you can do.

First, you need access to a law library. If you have a lawyer, try to use his or her books, but sometimes limitations of space or time prohibit that possibility. With a little effort you can find a law library open to the public. In many counties there is one either in or near the courthouse. Law schools have major collections, and some are open to the public. If necessary you can always consult your telephone directory or call the state attorney general, the clerk of the local court, or the local public library to locate the resources you need.

DIVORCE LAW: STATUTES, CASE LAW, AND CONSTITUTIONS

The laws that affect your particular divorce come from three sources: statutes, case law, and, to a lesser extent, state and federal constitutions. Statutes are the laws passed by the legislature. Case law consists of the body of law that is created when judges decide cases, and particularly when a trial court's decision is appealed and judges in appeals courts write decisions. Those written opinions define legal principles and the ways in which those principles should be applied to the facts of the case on appeal. The decision of some trial courts, and those of most appellate courts, are published by the state in case law books and are referred to as "official reports." Most of the officially reported current decisions also are published in a set called the *New York Supplement*. Constitutional law, as applied in New York divorces, is based on legal interpretations of both the U.S. and the New York State constitutions.

THE DOMESTIC RELATIONS LAW AND THE POCKET PART

Divorce cases are decided on the basis of (1) specific divorce statutes promulgated by the legislature, (2) more general legal principles, and (3) plain old common sense. Legislative enactments (statutes) are codified by number and then arranged by subject within a multivolume set of books. In New York they are found in the Domestic Relations Law, published as book fourteen of *McKinney's Consolidated Laws of New York Annotated.*

The index for the Domestic Relations Law is located at the end of the two-book set, which together comprise book fourteen. Thus, if you have a particular issue you want to research, such as the duty of a mother to provide child support, you would look under "support and support proceedings" and other words that come to mind when checking the index. You will then be referred to specifically numbered statutes bearing on the subject, which in this case would be section 32 of the Domestic Relations Law. Following each statute will be a summary of court cases interpreting the statutes. These "annotations," as they are called, are court decisions in which the meaning of the statute has been explained. These court decisions are considered "precedent," which subsequent courts will attempt to follow. If some cases in the annotations appear to be inconsistent it may be because different facts led different judges to apply the statute differently. When you have located the applicable statute, be sure to check the small supplement tucked into a pocket inside the back cover of the volume. This "pocket part" is periodically (usually annually) replaced to update the divorce volume. It reflects changes in statutes and later court decisions. In our child support example you would be misled if you did not check the pocket part, for the law has been amended to make mothers equally liable with fathers for support of their children since the hardcover *book fourteen* was printed.

CASES: NEW YORK SUPPLEMENT

After you have read the statutes, reviewed the annotations, and checked the pocket part for changes in the law or later cases, you will want to make a list of those cases bearing on the issue you are researching. To read these written decisions you must then turn to the "official reports" or, more likely in your library, the *New York Supplement.*

Finding the decisions you wish to read is simple. The citations in the annotations are nothing more than abbreviated titles of cases. Thus the citation to *Friederwitzer v. Friederwitzer*, 447 N.Y.S.2d 893, means that the case is found in the 447th volume of the second series of the *New York Supplement*, begining at page 893. Be careful to distinguish between the first and second series of the *New York Supplement*. If you want the second series, look for the "2" on the spine of the book.

When you have located the case you will need to become acquainted with its organizational format, which is in four phases. First you will see the case number of this court opinion, the names of the judges, and the date of the court's decision. Then, before the actual opinion of the court, you will find numbered annotations, a brief history of the case, including lower court decisions, and a summary of this court's decision. Third you will find listed the names of legal counsel for both parties. Finally there will be the decision itself.

The numbered annotations, called "headnotes" or "syllabuses," at the beginning of the report are concise principles of law that the *editor* compiling the volume has gleaned from the court decision. *They are not official statements by the court.* Rather they are an aid to the reader in spotting issues the court has dealt with in the case. The numbers by the headnotes correspond to specific paragraphs in the body of the opinion and will allow you to quickly turn to the critical part of the case in which you are interested.

SHEPARDIZING

Every week courts decide cases that limit, modify, or overrule older cases. Therefore, there is always a chance that the case that says everything you want has been affected by a recent decision. *Shepards' Citation* is an index devoted to keeping you informed of all recent cases affecting your case. Basically *Shepards'* picks up every subsequent case report that mentions the case you have just read. By following this research trail you will locate the most current judicial thinking on the case you originally started with. In the library, you will find that *Shepards'* currently has hardbound volumes for New York case citations up through at least 1989. More recent cases will be "Shepardized" (and found) in paperbound volumes. The most recent cases will be found in newsprint "slip" volumes.

To ensure that the cases you have found pertaining to your issues are still good law, you must Shepardize those cases. To do this you begin with the first volume that includes your case and work your way forward to the most recent slip volume. The *Shepards' Citation* also will list legal periodicals and treatises where the name of your reported case was mentioned. By reading the introductory pages of *Shepards' Citations* you will soon feel comfortable tracking down and researching these subsequent reports. Good lawyers Shepardize every case before using it in court, and if you are going to do your own legal research, you should do the same.

Other Aids

The most comprehensive aid to understanding New York divorce and family law (and consulting this is perhaps the better idea than reading the statutes and cases yourself) is *Law and the Family—New York.* this is a multivolume treatise written by Henry H. Foster, Jr., Doris Jonas Freed, and Joel R. Brandes. Annual supplements keep it up to date. It is written for lawyers, but it is lucid, comprehensive, and accurate. It is cited frequently by New York courts. The publisher is Lawyers Co-Operative Publishing Company of Rochester, New York. Other resources for your research include the following:

1. *Matrimonial Case Law—New York Edition*, by Willard H. DaSilva and Jay Landa, a looseleaf volume filled with concise statements of the main points in important court decisions.
2. *Nutshells*—short, readable volumes by West Publishing

Company on various areas of law from a national perspective. The *Family Law Nutshell* has helped many law students understand family law, and it might help you. Nutshells are inexpensive to buy but also can be found at most law libraries

3. *New York Digest*, 3d ed., which contains brief summaries of court decisions organized according to the issues of law involved. This can be very useful in helping you find, in the divorce sections, cases that are similar to yours.

CHAPTER SIX

---- ❖ ----

THE BASICS OF NEGOTIATIONS

BARGAINING IN THE SHADOW OF THE LAW

YOU HAVE decided to divorce, have chosen a lawyer or have
decided to represent yourself, and have gathered necessary
information on the family's economic situation. What happens now? Usually negotiations. This is not a totally new skill
you have to learn. We negotiate every day. Those who have
children know that a normal three-year-old is an instinctive
negotiator for the important things in life—staying up another
ten minutes, not eating the carrots until you promise candy,
and so forth. We each bargain and attempt to persuade in just
about every aspect of our relationships with other people,
and we also do so when we divorce.

In divorce, what do you negotiate? Potentially, everything.
Who pays whom and how much? Who gets the house? Who
gets custody of the children and who pays for college?

Except for those who ignore or boycott the divorce process
(or feel priced out of that market), the economic, custody,
and support issues in nine out of ten dead marriages in New
York are settled eventually by a private bargain between the
divorcing spouses rather than by a judge's decision after a
full-scale trial in court. Settlement is highly probable unless
one or both parties persist in being unreasonable, spiteful, or
determined to prove that he or she alone is "right."

59

The negotiations leading to agreement may take a week, they may take two years, or they may take even longer. The process may be businesslike and polite or it may be noisy, bitter, and interrupted by frequent trips to court. The husband and wife may do much of the bargaining directly, using their lawyers as advisers and draftsmen, or they may leave all of the face-to-face negotiating to the attorneys. They may use a mediator to assist them in their own direct negotiations, as described in chapter four. The bargaining may be completed before a lawsuit for divorce is even started; sometimes the parties do not settle until they are in the middle of a contested trial, after years of fighting. But the odds are that your case will in some way, at some time, be settled by you and your spouse rather than by a judge after a trial.

Many divorce judges, before and even during a trial, strongly encourage the couple to reach their own settlement and thus conserve court time. The judges recognize that the lawyers, who may have represented the parties for two years or more before trial, know much more about their clients, the clients' needs, and their resources than a judge will learn in a trial. A settlement drafted by the lawyers is therefore more likely to maximize total benefits than is a judge's decision.

In this chapter you will find basic information about negotiation techniques and strategy in divorce cases. There is an excellent *Yale Law Journal* article titled "Bargaining in the Shadow of the Law: The Case of Divorce." That title concisely states what a divorce case is often about, particularly where there is substantial property to be divided.

Divorce negotiations are "in the shadow of the law" in the sense that they are shaped partially by the parties' estimates of what a court will do if no agreement is reached and the case goes to trial. For instance, until 1980 the New York divorce law provided that a wife ordinarily had the right to receive alimony from her husband after a divorce but that no court could order a woman to pay alimony to her ex-husband, except in a case where he was about to go on welfare. The divorcing husband, therefore, had a very weak bargaining position when he asked his wife for financial help, even if she was rich and he had difficulty supporting himself. If she refused, the New York courts could not help him, since the law could not require a woman to pay alimony.

Under present New York law the court can require either spouse to pay maintenance (the term for what used to be called alimony), depending on the facts of the case. That gives the husband who has difficulty supporting himself more bargaining muscle. If his financially stronger wife refuses his request for support, he can force the case to trial and the judge will have the power to order the wife to pay maintenance.

So as we negotiate we look over our shoulder at what the court will do about property, maintenance, child support, and custody if you and your spouse do not reach a negotiated settlement. Obviously you need information about what a court would likely do if there were a contested trial. Your lawyer is your obvious source for those predictions. Most of the rest of this book focuses on giving you a general knowledge of the legal principles that New York courts use in deciding divorce cases and that your lawyer uses in predicting outcomes. That knowledge will empower you to participate more fully and more creatively with your attorney in negotiations. This chapter focuses on conventional adversary negotiations rather than the softer, problem-solving type negotiations, emphasizing the parties' emotional needs discussed in the chapter on mediation. The theory and technique of your own negotiations probably will be a blend of the two. Further, purer forms of both types of negotiations may be appropriate at different stages of the same case.

YOUR JOB

You have already listed the property you and your spouse have accumulated, itemized your income and expenses, and gathered other facts your lawyer requested. Now think of what you most want in a negotiated divorce settlement. Your initial answer on maintenance and child support and property may be "As much as I can get" or "As little as I can give," depending on your situation. Or it may be "I just want a fair result that ends the marriage and allows me to get on with my life quickly."

Perhaps you can be more specific. If it is already agreed that you are to have custody of the children, sole ownership of the house may be very important to you and for your (and the children's) emotional and financial security. You may need a high income for a few years until you complete your work for a graduate or professional degree. You may have a business that you want to protect from your spouse. Your most important need may be quite narrow: we once represented a woman whose first priority was protecting her job with a large company that her husband's friends owned and her husband operated. She had worked there for many years and her job gave her much personal satisfaction. Her age and background made it very difficult to move to as good a job with another employer, so she wanted to stay in her position even though her ex-husband would be her boss. We negotiated a deal that made it risky for her ex-husband to have her fired.

Look at your emotional attitudes toward the divorce and toward a negotiated settlement. Clients are prone to say things like "If you don't see that Jim is a horrible person, you aren't on my side." You may believe that your spouse is a miserable so-and-so, and by some objective criteria that may even be true. But if you feel you should use the divorce proceeding to punish your spouse for all of the bad things he or she has done to you, our strong recommendation is that you look at the costs of doing so, which we have outlined in earlier chapters.

YOUR ATTORNEY'S JOB

Your attorney should know New York divorce law, his or her way around in divorce courts, and the facts of your case. Using this knowledge he or she may predict for you what a court is likely to do after a trial. These predictions are often very difficult to make early in the case, for several reasons. First, the equitable distribution statute was passed by the New York legislature only in 1980 and amended since. It is still uncertain how the courts will interpret and apply many of its provisions. Second, the statute is complicated and gives the trial judge enormous discretion and flexibility in applying the law to the facts of an individual case. Third, your attorney may need time for a detailed investigation to gather important facts about your spouse's property and income or about how best to structure the custodial and visitation arrangements.

If you are doing your own negotiating you need whatever predictions your attorney can give you before getting into the custodial or financial aspects of your divorce. You also should get his or her advice on negotiating strategy and tactics. If your attorney is doing the negotiating you should discuss what you most want in a settlement, given the attorney's evaluation of what negotiating leverage you have. Whoever bargains, both you and your spouse should be clear on what your negotiating objectives and priorities are before starting the process.

You as a Negotiator

In our experience strong, rational client involvement in the negotiating process usually leads to better agreements because the client's preferences are more fully incorporated in the deal. You know what your needs are better than your attorney does. It's your life, and you should participate in the choices necessary in dividing property, in setting maintenance and child support, and in all other aspects of terminating the economic partnership that is part of your marriage.

We sometimes encourage our clients to negotiate the basic terms of divorce settlements directly with their spouses. This works best where there is approximate equality between husband and wife in bargaining ability and both want to reach an agreement. Many of our clients, particularly women, come to us wanting a champion and protector and do not feel inclined or equipped to participate directly in negotiations. We, of course, respect their wishes and do the negotiating personally, with frequent consultations with the client. Even when appropriate, direct participation in negotiations does not mean that the client writes the agreement or negotiates all of the details. The settlement agreement, particularly where large amounts of property have accumulated during the marriage, will be a complicated, technical document requiring good legal drafting. The husband and wife often can define the broad outlines of settlement for themselves—who gets custody, who gets the house, how much maintenance and child support will be awarded. After each discussion the couple has, we confer with our client to evaluate whether the tentative results of the negotiations are reasonable and to suggest additional issues that need to be resolved.

ANALYZING YOUR SPOUSE

You and your lawyer have discussed your wants and needs and the strengths and weaknesses of your case, and you are emotionally able to move toward a negotiated settlement. Now you should listen carefully as your spouse communicates his or her needs and analyze what you have that your spouse most wants. The idea is to give the other party something you have that is very important to him or her but less important to you. In return you get something that is more important to you than it is to your spouse. Let us illustrate with a hypothetical case, where ongoing negotiations cost unnecessary time and pain.

John and Ann's marriage clearly was over by the time John moved out of their house and went to live with his girlfriend. Ann sued for a divorce, then refused to go ahead unless John gave her more money than he felt he could pay. New York is among a minority of states where divorce still requires fault, such as adultery, abandonment, or cruelty by one of the parties, unless the parties reach an agreement. The vast majority of states bury a dead marriage at the unilateral request of one spouse who alleges "breakdown of the marriage," "incompatibility," or a similar no-fault ground.

Ann used New York's fault law as a negotiating tool and dropped her divorce suit after a year, even though the marriage clearly was over. She thought John's impatience for a divorce meant that she could get more money negotiating with him than a court would give her after a trial. John knew he could not get a fault divorce against Ann if she contested his lawsuit. Ann had good negotiating leverage; John wanted a divorce badly while Ann did not mind staying legally married, so long as she did not have to live with John. She used that leverage openly, telling him, "You can have your divorce anytime you want," so long as he first met her financial demands.

WHAT DOES HE OR SHE WANT?

Ann's cards were good, but she overplayed the hand and failed to make a quick deal. After two years of stalemate John was very frustrated at the law's failure to solve his problem and remained unwilling to give Ann as much money as she wanted. John considered moving to another state to get a no-fault divorce there, but decided against it. He then tried another approach, which was to give Ann what she didn't want—namely, John at home. He walked into the house and said, "Sweetie, you're right. We're married and I'm home." Ann left unhappily when John insisted on staying in the marital home that night and the following nights. His actions led to a property settlement after a few weeks and then to a divorce.

This illustrates several points. There was a good negotiating opportunity, but it was lost shortly after John left the house. Ann had something, the power to give John a divorce, which was very valuable to John and had little or no value in itself to Ann. It was reasonable for John to pay Ann something extra for a quick divorce, and initially he was willing to do so. A settlement would have allowed both parties to get on with their lives and avoid the stress on themselves and their children, which years of uncertainty and legal fighting always produce. The settlement opportunity passed, and John then forced the issue by doing something that he found unpleasant but that was even more unpleasant for Ann: returning home.

REMEMBER LONG-TERM COSTS AND BENEFITS

Again, keep in mind that where there are children, an ex-couple will continue to be involved with each other even after divorce. Support, custody, and visitation are ongoing processes, and negotiation or litigation tactics that leave one party or the other bitter may turn out to be quite expensive. If you both focus on giving your ex-partner what is comparatively more valuable to him or her and taking back what is comparatively more valuable to you, the chances are high that you will reach an agreement quickly and move on with your lives. But it takes two sides to negotiate, just as it takes two to fight. You should not allow yourself to be bullied or threatened as you negotiate your divorce agreement. If the other party tries to get an unfair agreement by intimidating you, you need to show firmness. Perhaps your resoluteness, and your attorney's, will change your spouse's attitude over time. Meanwhile, patience—and going to court for whatever temporary protections you need—is the proper strategy.

It also is wise not to box yourself in with ultimatums or written-in-stone positions. Have a clear idea of your interests and be creative and flexible in negotiating to advance those interests. Negotiation becomes difficult when the parties think in terms of absolutes and dictate terms to which they become glued.

Risk-Taking

Part of bargaining "in the shadow of the law" is knowing that if you and your spouse do not reach an agreement, a court is available to impose its solution on both of you. To illustrate some principles of risk taking in negotiations, here are some examples that ignore both the uncertainties usually present in real divorce cases and the noneconomic costs of matrimonial litigation we have discussed.

Imagine that you and your spouse have $100,000 to divide between you. Imagine further that if you cannot agree on how to divide the $100,000, the two of you will spend $20,000 of the $100,000 in lawyers' fees before a judge decides the case. Finally, imagine that both you and your spouse know that the judge probably would divide the remaining $80,000 evenly between you, so that after a trial you would each have $40,000.

If you conclude that the judge would divide the $80,000 evenly, why not agree between yourselves to divide the $100,000 equally, thus saving the $20,000 in lawyers' fees and other costs? You may do so, but it is quite rational for you to push for close to $60,000 of the $100,000. This is because your spouse knows that if there is no agreement and the case is litigated, he or she will get only $40,000; thus any settlement that gives him or her more than $40,000 is an economic improvement over the probable results after litigation. There is a $20,000 range in which both parties will get more by settlement than by litigation; dividing that $20,000 may require some pushing and shoving between the two of you. If one party insists on $55,000 and will not be moved, the other has the choice of taking $45,000 in a settlement or litigating and getting $40,000. The first spouse runs risks in demanding $55,000; the second may choose to give up $5,000 and litigate, perhaps even out of a spiteful desire to cost the first spouse the $15,000 difference between the $55,000 settlement demand and the $40,000 litigation result.

THE COIN FLIP

Your tolerance for uncertainty and risk may affect your success in negotiating such problems. Imagine that you had the choice between a sure $50 and a coin flip that would decide whether you took $100 or nothing. If you have a strong desire to choose the coin flip over the certain $50, you are a risk preferer in the situation. If you have a strong preference for taking the sure $50, you can be said to be risk averse. The risk preferer has an advantage over the risk-averse spouse in negotiations— for example, the dividing up of the $100,000 discussed above—for he or she has a greater tolerance for the possibility of losing. The risk-averse spouse may take the $45,000, particularly if he or she is convinced that the other party is comfortable with the risk that a deadlock will leave each with $40,000. The risk preferer will, other things being equal, be more inclined to push for the lion's share of the $20,000 at the risk of losing half of it. The risk-averse party will tend to settle for less than $50,000.

Whether you are risk averse or a risk preferer may depend not only on your psychological makeup but also on your economic abilty to tolerate the prospective loss. Herb Cohen, in his book *You Can Negotiate Anything*, illustrates the point. He frequently asks his audience how many would accept a bet where Cohen would pay $1,000,000 if a coin toss came up heads and the audience member would pay Cohen $100,000 if it were tails. Very few people offer to take the bet because very few people can afford to lose $100,000 at the toss of a coin, even if winning means $1,000,000. Cohen states that many would accept if the bet were $100 against $1,000 because most of us can afford to lose $100, and ten to one is a very good potential gain. Risk aversion may greatly diminish negotiating strength if the other side knows and chooses to exploit that aversion to risk.

TRIALS ARE ALWAYS RISKY

The inherent uncertainty in the judicial process gives the risk-preferring spouse an advantage over the risk-averse spouse. Your lawyer will give you his or her best estimates of what is likely to happen at trial, but New York courts have enormous discretion in divorce cases and the judge's decision may be quite different from your attorney's prediction, for better or for worse. You can avoid that uncertainty by reaching agreement now, but a relatively small tolerance for uncertainty may leave you needing an agreement more than your spouse does. One of the basic rules of commercial negotiations is that to make a good deal you should seem prepared to walk away without a deal. If your spouse knows that you cannot stand uncertainty and risk, he or she may insist on unfair concessions before giving you the certainty you want, the signing of a divorce settlement.

Finally, it is a cliché that a good settlement is one that completely satisfies neither party but with which each can live. If your side wins too much and the opposition gets too little, the whole agreement is more apt to come unhinged, and costly litigation may ensue. Where both sides feel that the terms are fair and reasonable and were arrived at by give-and-take, there is psychological and moral pressure to abide by the agreement, in much the same way you are honor-bound when you "shake on it." Studies have shown that where the parties arrive at support terms by negotiation and agreements, that are found by the court to be acceptable, the obligor pays, and pays on time, more frequently than when support terms are imposed on the obligor by a court. This word to the wise should be sufficient: avoid arrearage and enforcement problems if you can.

CHAPTER SEVEN

PROPERTY DIVISION

ON JULY 19, 1980, the Equitable Distribution Law became effective in New York State and the rules for divorcing spouses shifted massively. The law is still fairly new as statutes go, and many important questions about how it should be interpreted and applied have yet to be answered by our courts. We state what we believe the rules are or will be, based on existing New York court decisions and on the experience of other states with older and more settled marital property laws. Some knowledge of the pre-1980 rules may help you understand the present rules—and also why your aunt's 1979 divorce terms are not a very useful guide for current divorces.

THE OLD ORDER

Before the 1980 law became effective, marital property was only property that was titled in both names, such as a marital home owned "by the entireties" or a joint savings or bank account with "rights of survivorship." The old laws gave New York judges few powers to divide property between divorcing spouses. Imagine, for instance, that a husband had started and built up a restaurant chain during a twenty-year marriage while his wife stayed home with the children. The business was a corporation and he owned all of the stock. On divorce the wife had no claim to that property because title to the stock was not in her name. She could ask the court for alimony, and the court was required to order the husband to pay based on her needs and his ability to pay, but she was deprived of a share of the property accumulated during the marriage. The situation was even more unfair if the husband had little income and the accumulated property was in the wife's name, for New York courts also had no power to order a wife to pay alimony.

The old title system was inadequate, and many New York attorneys, including the authors of this book's introduction and Appendix B, worked for years for laws giving divorcing New York spouses property rights similar to those long enjoyed by citizens of community property and equitable distribution states. On alimony, the U.S. Supreme Court ruled in 1979 that statutes giving women, but not men, rights to seek alimony were unconstitutional, and so New York's old alimony statute became unenforceable.

The Revolution

Overnight, with the passage of the Equitable Distribution Law, New York's marital property law became one of the most sophisticated and progressive in the country. The statute enumerates thirteen factors that New York courts are to consider in distributing marital property and eleven factors to be used in deciding whether and how much maintenance is to be awarded to a spouse. The essential property concept is that marriage is an economic partnership, and that the property accumulated during a marriage is to be divided equitably on divorce, regardless of which spouse holds legal title. Men have gained equal rights with women to seek alimony, now called maintenance.

Appendix C contains the text of the Equitable Distribution Law; we suggest that you read it if you expect to be closely involved in negotiating property division or maintenance issues and to refer to it again as the need arises. Our explanation of the concepts and implications of marital property, separate property, maintenance, and other terms used in the statute will be more meaningful to you if you read the law itself. Again we return to our friends Mary Ellen and Jim for illustration of the principles involved.

CONTINUING SAGA

Mary Ellen returned to our office shortly after Jim moved out. She brought to this meeting the checklist discussed in Appendix D. The task of accounting for her monthly expenses was proving to be difficult. It was hard to focus on utility bills, insurance premiums, taxes, and the like. She wished she had been more familiar with those figures during her marriage. We had to assure her that although this exercise was difficult, it was essential. She said,

> Each time I sit down to attack those financial forms you gave me, my mind blurs. I just can't keep my thoughts straight. Then when I got to the questions about our insurance and Jim's pension plan, I knew I didn't have a clue! I felt so helpless. Jim and I plan to get together so he can help me list our assets.
>
> It's so mechanical and stark putting dollar values on sixteen years together, and dividing everything up. It's hard for me to do that when I'm still feeling so emotional.

We gave Mary Ellen information on the emotional stages of divorce (see chapter two, "The Psychological Divorce") to show that her feelings were not unusual. Nevertheless, she was told, our first priority was to assess the property to be divided. Until this was accomplished we would be without a clear picture of her future resources.

In New York, the premise of the New York marital property

and maintenance laws is that modern marriage should be viewed as a form of economic, as well as social, partnership. Therefore, all remaining assets acquired during the marriage by individual or joint efforts or expenditures should be equitably divided upon dissolution. It is the product of the marital partners' economic efforts that constitutes the kitty for equitable distribution. We assured her, however, that property division did not occur in a vacuum. Many factors are considered, including the future earning power of each spouse.

Mary Ellen was convinced that she could never find a job that would pay enough to allow her to adequately support herself and two teenagers. She loved her home and her neighborhood. Would this divorce cause her to lose her present lifestyle?

We emphasized again that this is why the division of property is one of the most critical aspects in the divorcing process. Two households are about to be created out of a single household, and in most families this demands changes in the living standards of both parents and their children. Mary Ellen wanted the house and some income-producing property to supplement the maintenance and child support she expected from Jim. She knew that owning property would make her feel more secure after the divorce.

DIVIDING MARITAL PROPERTY

Except in cases involving marriages of short duration, no children, and limited marital property, the task of property division is not easy, technically or emotionally. The current Equitable Distribution Law and the presence of tax problems require detailed accounting of the marital assets. The cold mathematical facts of property settlement often do not fit well with the emotional aspects of divorce.

Courts go through a four-step process to reach a full and fair division of the total assets, and individuals in negotiating or in mediating property division should go through a similar process. By completing a questionnaire we gave her, Mary Ellen and Jim got started on the first steps in the process:

1. Determine which property is "marital" under the statute and which property belongs solely to one party, making it separate, or nonmarital, property.
2. Value each significant item of property.
3. Consider how debts, attorney fees, and other closing-down expenses should be provided from the economic resources at hand.
4. In light of all of the above, and by applying the factors enumerated in the Equitable Distribution Law, the court will decide how to divide the marital assets most equitably. Sometimes an equitable result can be best achieved by providing for a "distributive award," re-quiring monthly or periodic payments from one spouse to the other, rather than by dividing a chunk of marital property. Under New York law, equitable doe not mean equal; it means fair, in view of all the circumstances.

MARITAL PROPERTY OR SEPARATE PROPERTY?

In New York courts, only marital property will be equitably divided between the spouses upon divorce. The separate property, as statutorily defined, of each party generally will remain that party's alone.

Generally speaking, *separate (or nonmarital) property* consists of all property acquired before the marriage and all property acquired after marriage by gift (except from the spouse), by inheritance, or as compensation for personal injuries. Sepa-rate property also usually includes property acquired in ex-change for other separate property and the increase in value of separate property (unless the nonowner spouse has con-tributed to the appreciation).

Marital property generally consists of *all* nonseparate property acquired during the marriage, unless there is a valid agreement between the spouses that provides otherwise. This includes all purchases made with the earnings of either or both, regardless of who holds legal title to the property. For instance, if the wife starts a real estate brokerage during the marriage, that business will be marital property, even though her husband does not have title to any stock in the business and even though only the wife's earnings went into starting the business.

New York courts view the marriage as a partnership, so that any assets accumulated during the marriage are presumed to be marital property. Therefore, those accumulations produced by individual or joint efforts or expenditures should be shared equitably upon the termination of that relationship by divorce or annulment. Separate property remains with the owner spouse, though the court may allow the spouse with custody of the children to occupy the marital home during the children's minority even though that home is techically the separate property of the other spouse.

Property acquired after the parties sign a separation agreement or after one of the parties starts a matrimonial lawsuit, but before their marriage is dissolved, generally is regarded as the separate property of the spouse who acquired it. The rationale is that the spouses are no longer working together in the interest of the marriage partnership.

You Can Decide

Spouses are legally authorized to determine the character, or definition, of their assets for themselves. That is, they may agree on what is marital property and what is separate property, and the courts will honor that agreement even though it gives a result that differs from what a judge would decide in a trial under the Equitable Distribution Law. To make these personal agreements enforceable they must be in writing and signed by the parties with all the formalities required for a deed. The agreement will be enforced by the divorce court, whether it was entered into before or after the parties married, as long as it was "fair and reasonable" when made and "not unconscionable" at the time the court divorces the parties.

By such agreements spouses also can change the status of their property at any time. For example, a husband may wish to make a gift of the family home to his wife. Courts generally uphold a couple's rights to contract with each other to make marital property into separate property; but when the spouses later divorce, the courts will take a very close look to make sure that the former marital property is now truly separate. Usually the burden of proof will be on the spouse who at the time of divorce is displeased with the definition of the property. He or she may argue that the transfer was part of a larger estate plan or was made for protection against creditors. In the absence of agreement otherwise, the statute says that gifts between spouses are marital property.

Mary Ellen, for example, always wore one truly lovely diamond ring. The ring had been left to Jim upon his grandmother's death. Mary Ellen had enjoyed wearing it for the ten years preceding the breakup. Did this ring constitute Jim's separate property? Possibly—unless Jim had given it to her at the right time and in the right way. If Jim had given the ring to Mary Ellen before they married, it would be her separate property. If he had given it to her after they married, it would be marital property, because gifts from one spouse to the other are marital property unless there is a formal written agreement otherwise.

SEPARATE PROPERTY IMPROVEMENTS AND INCOME

As a general rule, any income or increases in value attributable to separate property during marriage remain the separate property of the owner spouse. However, some New York courts have ruled that if separate property increases in value during marriage because of the owner spouse's active management or the indirect or the direct contributions of the nonowner spouse, the increase in value becomes marital property. Income from separate property, and the property itself, may be considered in determining a fair and equitable division of all property. For instance, if the court realizes that one spouse will be receiving monthly income from a separate property trust fund and the other spouse has no separate property, it will tend to award the second spouse a larger portion of the marital property than it would otherwise. If one spouse directly contributes to an increase in value of the other spouse's separate property, then the appreciation due to the nonowner spouse's efforts or expenditures clearly becomes marital property. Examples might be the husband who served as the unpaid carpenter for renovation of a building his wife had purchased before the marriage, or the wife who served as the unpaid decorator on a home owned by her husband. Moreover, New York decisions hold that spousal contributions in general, such as keeping the home and raising the couple's children, qualify a spouse for a share of the appreciation of the other's separate property if the appreciation resulted from the efforts of the owner spouse.

VALUING YOUR PROPERTY

Every item of property has its value. Spousal agreement as to the value of property can be a difficult but not insumountable task. Just as one person's junk is another's antique, certain items of personal property may have a very high value to one spouse.

On the birth of their first child, Jim gave Mary Ellen a solitaire diamond, which cost $3,000. He thought that the diamond probably was worth at least $4,000 today; for sentimental reasons, Mary Ellen felt it to be beyond price. Imagine their surprise when the gemologist put its market value at $2,500. Mary Ellen held that the ring should not even be considered part of their property settlement—after all, it had been a gift from Jim. Negotiations almost broke down when

Jim insisted it be valued and put into the marital property kitty. Eventually Mary Ellen "bought" the diamond from Jim at market value by giving him an offset against other marital property.

Divorcing couples often let sentiment cloud their judgment when valuing their assets. They each view their accumulations, whether a residence or a bird cage, as somehow intrinsically part of themselves and therefore not to be parted with, except at great price to their spouse. Louise Raggio tells the story of a $5 million settlement that was collapsing because both spouses insisted on having the one chain saw in their garage. Louise went out to a hardware store and bought a second, identical chain saw. The parties laughed at themselves and then signed the agreement. I have seen carefully drafted, complex million-dollar settlements evaporate over the disputed value of a dining table or a set of encyclopedias. To paraphrase the poet Robert Burns, would that we could see ourselves as others see us—when we wrangle over the bird cage.

MINIMIZING THE VALUATION DIFFICULTY

To the extent that he or she can, each individual should sit down and rationally set market values on all of the marital personal property (furniture, appliances, jewelry, and so on). If their figures do not agree, each should state the value to himself or herself of the item. The high bidder can then take the item from the marital property pot at the high bid price, resulting in a credit to the other spouse at that value. Imagine the husband's shocked expression when, after he has self-servingly stated a $10,000 value on household furnishings actually worth $4,000, the wife responds "All right, I'll take the cash, you keep the furniture." It's surprising how close this bidding process comes to setting a true market value on these personal items.

Once sentiment is removed from the process of valuation, the couple should be able to determine a reasonable value for most of their personal property. In valuing furniture and other household items, they should be guided not by what they paid for the item but by what it would sell for in the marketplace. (Some call this "garage sale" value, especially when it applies to used furniture.)

Market value is technically defined as the amount of money that a buyer (who is willing but not obligated to buy) would pay an owner (who is willing but not obligated to sell) for a particular piece of property. Market value is *not* the amount of money required to replace the item, nor is it what the item might bring at a distress or liquidation sale.

Costly or rare items of property, such as the residence, acreage, expensive jewelry, antiques, and paintings, probably will require the services of an appraiser for proper valuation. Even then, a mathematically precise valuation is impossible because appraisers (like lawyers and spouses) can honestly disagree. Nonetheless, the court will require present values based on the realities of the marketplace. The owner may give the court his or her opinion on an item's value. But the professional appraiser's opinion, supported with facts, figures, and particularly information on recent sales of comparable properties, probably will carry more weight with the court.

Special Considerations Affecting Value: Taxes, Sales Costs

For many items of property, particularly realty, the cost of selling the property should be considered when fixing its net value. If, for example, a home is to be sold, the net equity will be reduced by the broker's commission, attorneys' fees, and other closing costs.

The court also may consider reducing the market value of an item by the amount of taxes that might be incurred upon a subsequent sale. An example would be two shares of a corporation's stock, one purchased early in the marriage at a lower price, the other purchased later on in the marriage at a higher price. If Mary Ellen took the share purchased at the lower price and then she and Jim each sold, Mary Ellen would net less than Jim, even though they sold at the same time and at the same market price, assuming that their marginal tax rates were equal. This is because the capital gains tax on Mary Ellen's sale would be greater than the tax on Jim's sale, since she had a lower tax basis on her stock than Jim had on his. *Taxes affect the sale of most items.*

For example, New York State and possibly local taxes are imposed on the transfer of any interest in real property. This tax ranges from .4 percent ($4 for every $1,000) to over 11 percent, depending on where the property is and the value of interest being transferred. The tax is imposed even though the transfer is pursuant to a court order or a separation agreement, and the tax is collected when you file the deed, or in the case of a cooperative apartment, when the co-op registers the stock in your name. This is a very important factor to consider, as the tax is significant and must be paid when you are in the midst of an economically difficult situation. If you do not pay the tax at the time of the transfer you will be subject to substantial penalties when you do pay. Sooner or later you will pay, because sooner or later you will want to transfer (sell) the property to someone else.

You may be tempted to avoid the tax by failing to file the deed or by not registering your stock with the corporation. You should resist this temptation, for two reasons. First, it won't work. When you sell the property you will have to establish your ownership of it. That means you will have to file your deed or register your stock and pay the taxes then. However, your filing will be late, and penalties (more than 25 percent) will be collected. Second, as long as the public record reflects not your ownership but your former spouse's, the property will remain subject to his or her creditors. Even if they do not sell the property, you might have to pay them off out of your own pocket when you sell the property.

Not all tax news on this front is bad. A properly structured transfer between you and your spouse will not be subject to income taxes or capital gains taxes. In any event, you should consult a competent tax adviser before finalizing your agreement.

Taxes not only affect the transfer of real property, but they can affect the value of other property as well. We told Mary Ellen that she needs to establish the value of the couple's pension (retirement) plans. She needs to be sure that the value takes into account that taxes will need to be paid on the amounts that she receives from these plans and accounts. The calculation is a bit sophisticated and we recommend that a tax accountant be retained to establish the amounts involved.

Income tax matters must be considered as well. People getting divorced change not only their social status, but their tax status as well. Commonly asked questions concern filing status (joint or separate), claiming the children as dependents, maintenance as income and/or a deduction, transfer of the home, and the transfer of pension plan assets and IRAs.

JOINT OR SEPARATE FILING STATUS

Although you will be separated at the end of a tax year, you may have the option to file a joint return with your spouse or a married but separate return. The choice of one over the other is basically a matter of arithmetic. The option that creates the least tax liability for you or the greatest refund is the method of choice. Unless you have previously agreed to file a certain way, the filing of a joint return will require the agreement of both spouses. Consequently, it is something that should be included in the separation agreement. Of course, if you are divorced the option of joint filing status is unavailable.

Should you opt for joint filing, and if your spouse is the one having the return prepared, you should be cautious in reviewing the return before you sign it. It is no surprise that in the months immediately following your separation cash will be tight, or at least it will seem that way. People often react to this circumstance by squeezing every penny they can at every opportunity. An inflated deduction here, an omitted item of income there—sooner or later it can add up to a significant amount of money. It also can add up to significant trouble. Your signature on the return makes you just as liable for the information contained in the return as your spouse, whether you prepared it or not and whether or not it was your income or deduction that comes into question.

WHO GETS THE DEPENDENTS?

Until a few years ago this question was answered by resorting to shoeboxes full of receipts, canceled checks, and assorted financial memorabilia. Parents were constantly able to enter into conflict concerning who paid how much, when, and for what in order to establish an entitlement to this exemption. Two areas of change have reduced the conflict potential.

First of all, for taxpayers in the higher-income brackets the exemption is being phased out entirely. As long as this process continues, the value of the exemption may not be of any interest to the higher-income party. Tax laws do have a way of changing, however, so the door should be left open in order to capitalize on any future change that could restore the value of the exemption.

Second, under current law the custodial parent gets the exemption unless he or she relinquishes it in writing to the other parent.

IS MAINTENANCE TAXABLE INCOME? IS IT DEDUCTIBLE FROM INCOME?

Maintenance can be deductible from the gross income of the paying spouse and included in the gross income of the recipient spouse. But the parties must do it right to accomplish that result. The paying spouse often wants the payments classified as maintenance, while the recipient prefers the payments be classified as anything else. We suggest that a knee-jerk response to this issue is at best shortsighted and could be costly. The parties should be mindful that there is a limited amount of dollars available to allocate. By shifting the tax burden between taxpayers of different brackets, parties can end up maximizing the supply of these dollars. Careful consideration of this issue should be the rule, with input from a qualified tax professional.

Assuming that it is determined that maintenance should be paid so that the payments are deductible to the payor and includable as income to the recipient, the following requirements must be satisfied:

1. The obligation to pay maintenance must arise from a decree or judgment of divorce or a "separation instrument." If, before you have finalized your agreement, you realize that support payments need to be made, it might be to your advantage to consider entering into written temporary support agreement.
2. These payments must be made either to your spouse or for his or her "benefit." This means that the agreement can provide that the payments be made to a third party (like a mortgage company or medical care providers) and still be considered deductible.
3. The payments must be made in "cash." Checks or money orders are acceptable according to IRS regulations.
4. The agreement must provide that the payments will not continue past the time of the recipient's death.
5. The payor and the recipient cannot be members of the same household when the payments are made. A regulation does state that the parties can live in the same house for one month while one party prepares to move out.

WILLS

Perhaps you are among the people with the foresight to have drawn up a will while you were married. If so, your will may state something like: "If I die my estate goes to my husband . . ." If you are seeking a divorce, it is likely that you would prefer that your soon-to-be ex not inherit your entire estate. In order to avoid this result you should make a new one, revoking the old one. However, as long as you are not divorced or without a formal waiver of certain rights, your spouse will continue to be a factor in your estate. If you are legally married and do not have an enforceable court decree or a waiver of inheritance rights in a properly executed agreement, your spouse will have the right to elect to take one-third of your estate or $50,000, whichever is greater. In addition, without the proper paperwork you will be unable to remove your spouse as a death beneficiary on your pension plan. Although there is little you can do about the pension, you can lessen (but not eliminate) your spouse's claim on your estate by a properly drawn will.

If you have no will and no children, your entire estate will go to your spouse. If you have no will and you have children, your estate will be split between your spouse and your children ($50,000 plus half of the balance to your spouse and the rest to the children). If your children are minors, your spouse may attempt to qualify to manage the children's money. If you fear that situation, you should consider establishing a trust for your children in a new will and appointing a trustee of your choice.

If You Can't Agree, the Court Will Decide

If the spouses, either directly or through their attorneys, cannot agree on the division of their marital assets, the court will complete the task, guided by the legal principles of equity and fairness contained in the Equitable Distribution Law. This does not necessarily mean that there will be an equal division of the assets. As we have said, equality is not always equity. The Equitable Distribution Law provides that the court, in granting a divorce, must distribute the marital property between the spouses and that it shall do so "considering the circumstances of the case and of the respective parties" as well as the statutory guidelines.

THE BIG THIRTEEN OF MARITAL PROPERTY DISTRIBUTION

The thirteen factors listed in the marital property distribution portion of the Equitable Distribution Law must be weighed and balanced by a judge when he or she divides and distributes marital property after a divorce trial. Each of the thirteen factors may have more or less value or weight, depending on the case's overall circumstances. We will therefore briefly discuss each of the thirteen factors that a court is required by law to consider in distributing marital property.

"(1) *the income and property of each party at the time of marriage, and at the time of the commencement of the action.*"
The divorce court has the power to distribute only marital property; it must leave separate property with the spouse who has it. But factor one permits the court to give the spouse who has less separate property a greater share of the marital property. Imagine that a husband inherited a fortune during the marriage and the parties accumulated a much smaller sum as marital property during marriage. A court, using factor one, would tend to give most of the marital property to the wife because she has less separate property.

"(2) *the duration of the marriage and the age and health of both parties.*"
Where only one spouse earned significant income during the marriage while the other, typically the wife, stayed home with the couple's children, the court will tend to increase the wife's share according to the length of the marriage. In a long marriage, say twenty years or more, where the wife has devoted herself to the home and to supporting the husband's business activities, factor two would influence the court toward giving more of the accumulated marital property to the

wife. Similarly, if the wife is relatively old for the job market or in poor health and so less able to become economically self-supporting, the court will tend to give her more marital property.

"(3) the need of a custodial parent to occupy or own the marital residence and to use or own its household effects."

If the wife has primary custody of minor children, the court will tend to give her possession and occupancy, and in some cases ownership, of the spouses' marital home. This is for the benefit of the children as well as their mother, as it may lessen the traumatic dislocations and uncertainties that divorce brings for children. Of course, if the father gets custody, the court will want to give him possession and occupancy of the house. Where the house is owned jointly, the court may order it sold when the children reach majority and the net proceeds to be divided.

"(4) the loss of inheritance and pension rights upon dissolution of the marriage as of the date of dissolution."

During marriage, each spouse has the right to take part of the other's estate upon death, regardless of what the deceased spouse's will provides. Similarly, many pension plans give important rights to a surviving spouse. These contingent economic benefits are lost upon divorce. Therefore the court will lean toward giving more marital property to the poorer spouse and the one with smaller accumulated pension benefits.

"(5) any award of maintenance under subdivision six of this part."

If one spouse is paying maintenance to the other, the recipient has less need for income from property. Conversely, the spouse paying maintenance may need more property to generate the income needed to pay the maintenance, so the statute instructs the court to consider maintenance and marital property division together in an attempt to reach an overall economic result that is just.

"(6) any equitable claim to, interest in, or direct or indirect contribution made to the acquisition of such marital property by the party not having title, including joint efforts or expenditures and contributions and services as a spouse, parent, wage earner and homemaker, and to the career or career potential of the other party."

Factor six is the key issue in many equitable distribution cases. Assume that the wife worked while the husband earned his M.B.A. She then stayed at home with the children while he built his own consulting business and accumulated investment properties, title to which was taken in his name alone. Assume further that the wife frequently acted as the unpaid bookkeeper, office manager, and hostess for the husband's business associates. At divorce it is fair for the court to lean the wife's way in passing out the stocks, bonds, land, and so forth that the husband's business has generated. The husband will keep getting income from his skills and his personal business contacts after the divorce, but the wife can get a return on her "investment" in his education, skills, and business contacts only through maintenance or through getting a bigger share of the distributable marital property.

"(7) the liquid or nonliquid character of all marital property."

The husband may have built up a profitable business during the marriage with assets that cannot be sold quickly for their full value, or, for instance, there might be corporate stock that is restricted and cannot be sold publicly until years after it was issued. The court may give full value to those assets, leave them with the owner spouse, and compensate the other spouse either with more easily transferable marital property or with a "distributive award."

The drafters of the Equitable Distribution Law created an innovative and flexible distributive award device. A court can balance its grant to a husband of a business considered marital property with an order that the husband pay a certain sum of money, either all at once or in installments, to the wife at or after the divorce, to compensate for her not being granted any portion of the business. Those payments are intended by the law to be part of, to supplement, or to substitute for the distribution of marital property and, therefore, not to be taxable income to the wife, as maintenance payments would be.

"(8) the probable future financial circumstances of each party."

If the wife has devoted herself to the home and to furthering the husband's career instead of developing her own earning potential, it makes sense to give her more of the marital property. She will have more difficulty accumulating new property than the husband will. On the other hand, if one spouse has a large amount of separate property, from inheritance or whatever source, that guarantees his or her future financial security, the court may tend to give the poorer spouse more of the accumulated marital property.

"(9) the impossibility or difficulty of evaluating any component asset or any interest in a business, corporation or profession, and the economic desirability of retaining such asset or interest intact and free from any claim or interference by the other party."

In the consulting business case used in discussing factor six, the husband's M.B.A., skills, and personal business contacts are important assets because they greatly increase his earning power. But they cannot be transferred to the wife or to any third party who might want to buy them, and thus they do not have an exchange value. The business may have goodwill value because the husband has been consulting for years and has a large number of customers who keep coming back to him and referring others. But that goodwill may not be fully transferable, because the customers are personally loyal to the husband.

The court cannot transfer any portion of the husband's education, skills, or business contacts to the wife. Nor would it be sensible for the court to require the husband to sell his business, even if it could be sold, and divide the proceeds, since the wife's and the children's future support may depend on the husband's ability to earn income from his business. What the court can do is give the wife an extra share of other marital property or a distributive award, as discussed in factor seven.

"(10) the tax consequences to each party."

Factor ten was added by the 1986 amendment, although previously it was considered under former catch-all factor ten. The amendment simply makes tax consequences an *express* statutory factor. One party may have a higher marginal tax rate after the divorce than the other, and both parties may come off better in an arrangement in which taxable income is shifted to the spouse with the lower tax rate. For instance, where there are two pieces of property, each worth $10,000, but one property has a tax basis of $2,000 and the other has a tax basis of $7,000, it makes sense to give the first to the spouse who will likely have the lower tax rate when the assets are sold. In that way the overall taxes are cut down. However, the spouse taking the asset with the higher tax liability should expect to be compensated elsewhere in the economic divorce package.

"(11) the wasteful dissipation of assets by either spouse."

This factor also was added by the 1986 amendment to the Equitable Distribution Law and merely expresses in statutory form the holdings of prior cases. Note, however, that the word *assets* is not qualified by a term such as "family" or "marital" and, if broadly construed, may include separate assets. In any event, an extravagant wife or a gambler husband may be penalized by the application of this factor.

"(12) any transfer or encumbrance made in contemplation of a matrimonial action without fair consideration."

Again, the 1986 amendment merely expresses the prior New York decisions and holdings on this issue. For example, a husband may not strip himself of assets by giving them to a lover or relative in order to make a smaller property distribution or in the hope of reducing maintenance.

"(13) *any other factor which the court shall expressly find to be just and proper.*"

This is former catch-all factor ten, which has been renumbered thirteen and is intended to cover situations not covered by the other enumerated factors.

DIVIDING THE INDIVISIBLE: SPECIAL ASSETS

By their nature, some assets are not easily divisible. If the court must award a specific asset to one of the spouses, provisions are made to compensate the other. What cannot be divided can often be traded.

The jointly owned family residence is usually an indivisible asset. Most courts will award possession and occupancy of the family home to the spouse having custody of the children. This is done partly in an attempt to minimize further disruption of the children's lives. Therefore, if there is no additional property of equal value to effect a trade-off with the noncustodial spouse, the custodial spouse may receive exclusive possession of the home for a number of years, on the understanding that the residence will then be sold and the net proceeds of the sale be divided equally between the spouses. In the meantime, the noncustodial spouse might be given a compensating lien against the residence. The divorce judgment often provides that the home will be sold, should the custodial parent remarry, enter a cohabitation relationship, no longer use the home as his or her primary residence, or die, whichever occurs first.

Pensions and retirement benefits may be forms of deferred compensation in which there is a spousal interest that should be valued in the event of divorce. Moreover, pensions are the largest marital assets for many divorcing couples. Often an actuary will be necessary to determine the value of each specific plan. Pensions or other entitlements of employment often will be allocated to the employee spouse, while other marital property is given as a setoff to the nonemployee spouse. Or the court may require that pension benefits be divided "if, as, and when" received by the employee spouse. If the pension rights are not to be divided as received in the future, then the court will determine the present value of the pension rights and factor it into the marital property distribution.

Business Goodwill

Goodwill is property of an intangible nature, and it is often relevant for divorcing professionals. The accountant, dentist, eye doctor, lawyer, or whatever, by virtue of training and past performance, may have established a professional practice that promises a good future income. The nonprofessional spouse has been a silent partner in building the practice and is now forced to withdraw from the partnership. The valuing of goodwill invariably requires the services of an expert, usually an accountant, an economist, or a business broker experienced in selling professional practices. A business such as Jim's medical equipment corporation also may have goodwill that an appraiser will consider in appraising its value.

Professional Licenses: O'Brien v. O'Brien

If one spouse becomes a doctor during the marriage, is the professional license marital property? New York's highest court said yes in the case of O'Brien v. O'Brien, published in December 1985. Most other states say no, often on the grounds that a professional degree or license is not property, since it cannot be transferred from the license holder to another person. The legal principles that New York's court of appeals announced in O'Brien apply to licenses to practice law, accounting, dentistry, and other professions. We will review briefly the facts in Dr. and Mrs. O'Brien's marriage as an aid to applying those legal principles to other situations.

The trial court found that nearly all of the O'Briens' nine-year marriage was devoted to the husband's obtaining a license to practice medicine. When the two married they were both teachers. Shortly after the marriage the husband returned to college to complete his bachelor's degree and sufficient premedical courses to enter medical school. The couple then moved to Mexico for three and one-half years, during which the husband attended medical school and the wife worked to pay the couple's expenses. They then returned to New York, where the wife resumed her teaching career and the husband completed the school and internship work necessary for his license to practice medicine. Two months after Dr. O'Brien got that license he started a divorce suit against Mrs. O'Brien. At trial Mrs. O'Brien claimed that the license was marital property and that she should receive part of its value. The court of appeals agreed.

The O'Brien decision noted that New York's Equitable Distribution Law is premised on the idea that a marriage is, among other things, "an economic partnership" and said: "As this case demonstrates, few undertakings during a marriage better qualify as the type of joint effort that the statute's economic partnership theory is intended to address than contributions toward one spouse's acquisition of a professional license."

HOW DO WE VALUE A PROFESSIONAL LICENSE?

Once it was decided that the license was marital property, the next question was how to value it. The court of appeals held that a professional license's value "is the enhanced earning capacity it affords the holder." At trial an expert for Mrs. O'Brien had testified that Dr. O'Brien's license was worth $472,000, that being the present value of the higher earnings the expert estimated Dr. O'Brien would enjoy because of his having medical training and his license. The trial court ordered Dr. O'Brien to pay Mrs. O'Brien 40 percent of that value, or

$188,000, in eleven annual installments. Since the O'Briens had no children and Mrs. O'Brien was capable of supporting herself by her teaching, there was no child support or maintenance to be paid from Dr. O'Brien's future earnings.

The *O'Brien* concept that a professional license acquired by one spouse during marriage is marital property, and that its value can be divided between the spouses by a divorce court, will enormously complicate the valuation and division of marital property for many couples. What should a court do if one spouse earned a professional degree early in the marriage and each spouse has enjoyed the professional's higher earnings and property accumulations for twenty years before divorce? How does a court avoid double-counting, that is, requiring the professional spouse to pay the other a portion of the present value of the license and also requiring higher maintenance and child support because of the professional's higher future earning ability? Courts have much discretion under the Equitable Distribution Law, and we expect that for years to come it will be very difficult to predict the outcome of a New York divorce trial involving a professional license. Some recent New York decisions have held that where there is a "track record" as to professional earnings, that record should be the basis for valuing a professional practice, and that the value of the license merges into the value of the practice.

BEYOND *O'BRIEN*

The principles of O'Brien have been used to dramatically expand traditional notions of property. Celebrity status, career enhancement, and professional fellowships and certifications all can be classified as marital property and therefore be valued and divided. Some knowledge of the facts in some of the more recent cases is useful in understanding the legal concepts being applied.

In the case of *Elkus v. Elkus* the court considered the position of a husband who devoted himself to the advancement of his wife's singing career. He taught her, critiqued her, supported and coached her. In addition he cared for the parties' children. All the while the wife's career flourished to where she became a world-renowned star and celebrity. The increase in her earning capacity during the years of marriage was marital property, despite the fact that the wife did not receive a license, permit, or certificate.

In the case of McAlpine v. McAlpine the parties disputed the status of the husband's fellowship in the Society of Actuaries. By the time the parties married, the husband already had completed many of the prerequisites for the fellowship. However, during the marriage he passed five of the ten required examinations. During the period after the marriage the husband worked full time and studied at home on his own to prepare for the examinations. The wife, however, rendered no assistance to him and suffered no sacrifices as a result of the husband's efforts. The husband performed most of the household chores as well. The court acknowledged that the fellowship was a valuable asset and it was acquired during the marriage. Therefore it was marital property.

That did not end the matter for Mr. and Mrs. McAlpine. The fact that something is determined to be marital property does not necessarily mean that its value will be divided between the spouses. In Elkus, after ruling that the career enhancement was marital property, the court ordered that the enhancement be valued and shared. In McAlpine, although the career enhancement was determined to be marital property, the wife was not entitled to share the benefits because she was unable to show any contribution toward her husband's obtaining the fellowship.

These two cases illustrate two important concepts. First of all, marital property is an elastic concept. Second, there are principles of fairness laid out in New York's equitable distribution law that judges use in dividing marital property.

Your Stamp Collection

Specific items of marital property may have great sentimental value to one spouse or the other. The court will attempt to award to each party the items in which he or she has a personal interest, such as sporting goods, tools, and special collections. The court also will try to allocate items that common sense dictates should be awarded to one party: a library used by only one of them, jewelry worn by the other. In general the court will take into account the reasonable expressed wishes of each individual.

Some of the questions in the following checklist may be applicable to your own situation. Many of the issues are sophisticated and will, no doubt, require professional assistance to resolve.

Checklist for Property Division

1. If you own a home, who is named on the title? Are there any other parcels of real property or stock ownership in a cooperative corporation? What is the title status? Are there any mortgages, liens, or encumbrances on the title? Who will asssume which obligations?
2. Have the taxes been paid? What tax consequences will occur from any transfer of interest in real estate? If property other than real estate is to be sold, what are the tax consequences there? Will an appraiser be required to value the property? Who will pay for the cost of the appraisal?
3. If you are living in a rental apartment, is there a lease? In whose name is it leased? When does the lease expire? Is the building likely to become a cooperative or a condominium? Who is to continue occupying the apartment? Who is to pay the rent? Is the lease assignable? Is it to be assigned? If there is a deposit, who is to receive that?
4. Is it necessary to dispose of a business? If so, should the value of the business be appraised? Is the busines

a partnership? Is the spouse a partner? If so, is that interest to be purchased by the other spouse? Is the business incorporated? Are both spouses officers or directors? Is one to resign? If both are stockholders, what disposition is to be made of the holdings? If one is a creditor, what disposition is to be made of that claim?

5. Does the business or professional practice have good-will value? Did either spouse acquire a professional license or educational degree or otherwise substantially increase his or her earning capacity during the marriage? How should the goodwill or the enhanced earning capacity be valued?

6. Is one spouse holding in his or her name any separate property belonging to the other spouse? If so, is he or she to retain it?

7. Is there any insurance on personal items—jewelry, furs, cameras, and so forth? Are any of the policies to be transferred?

8. Does either of the parties have an interest in any profit-sharing plans, pension plans, or other retirement funds? Are they fully or partially vested? Will an actuary be required? What disposition is to be made of these interests? Why?

9. Does either spouse owe the other any money? Is there an outstanding note or other evidence of the debt? How is the indebtedness to be treated?

10. Are you and your spouse jointly liable on any obligation? If so, what happens when the obligation matures? Is one spouse to assume the debt and indemnify the other?

11. Is there any litigation pending between the spouses in addition to the divorce proceeding? Is there any other pending litigation in which one or both of you are involved, either as a plaintiff or as a defendant?

12. Are there any outstanding bills or obligations that were incurred by one spouse but for which the other is or may be liable? Who is to discharge that obligation? Is there to be indemnification?

13. When should credit cards and accounts be canceled and surrendered? Can each spouse's credit be preserved by opening new accounts?

14. Are schedules to be prepared, listing exact debts each spouse is to assume and pay?

15. Have the parties filed any joint income tax returns in the past? If there is a refund, who is to get it? If there is a deficiency assessment, who is to pay it? Is one spouse to indemnify the other as to any liability regarding prior income tax returns?

16. Who is responsible for other tax matters, such as estate taxes, corporation returns, and partnership returns?

17. Are authenticated copies of future tax returns to be exchanged?

18. Is each party to waive his or her rights in the estate of the other?

19. Has either party an existing will in which the other is named executor or executrix, devisee, or legatee? Should this be changed?

20. Should either spouse be required to leave the other or the children a specific sum or sums by will or is that spouse's estate to be charged for future support, medical obligations, and so forth?

21. Are there revocable "living trusts" that should be changed because of the altered marital relationship?

22. Are the children beneficiaries under any existing testamentary or living trust? Should they be? Which parent is to receive and control the income on the children's behalf?

23. Is the spouse's maintenance obligation (assuming there are continuing payments) to survive death and be binding upon his or her estate? If so, may the obligation be capitalized so that the estate may be promptly closed?

24. Is a spouse to furnish any security for the performance of his or her obligations under the agreement? If so, what form will the security take?

CHAPTER EIGHT

SPOUSAL
MAINTENANCE

UNTIL 1980, New York statutes permitted awards of alimony only to "innocent" wives who had not committed acts that gave their husbands fault grounds for divorce. Husbands could not get alimony regardless of the circumstances. Only in a nondivorce situation in family court was it theoretically possible to impose a support obligation on a wife, in order to keep the husband off public assistance.

In addition to the alimony-is-only-for-wives characteristic of New York law before 1980, it was more difficult for husbands than it was for wives, under comparable circumstances, to obtain a divorce on fault grounds such as adultery, abandonment, or cruelty, especially if the marriage had been of long duration (about eighteen or twenty years). New York courts made fault divorces harder for husbands to get because a fault divorce against the wife meant that she couldn't get alimony, whatever her need.

The enactment of the Equitable Distribution Law in 1980 changed much of that. Maintenance, the new term for alimony, formerly was awarded primarily on the economic basis of reasonable needs and ability to pay. The 1986 amendment to the 1980 statute, however, shifted some emphasis to the standard of living maintained during the marriage. It may be awarded to a husband as well as to a wife, and it may be permanent or temporary. The marital fault of a wife no longer is an automatic bar to alimony; now only behavior so bad that it shocks the court's conscience is relevant in awarding maintenance (or in the distribution of marital property). The new law requires the divorce court to consider eleven factors (similar to but not the same as the thirteen factors used in dividing marital property) in deciding the amount and duration of maintenance. Those factors are listed in Appendix C under number six, "Maintenance." Back to Mary Ellen.

EACH SPOUSE IS FINANCIALLY RESPONSIBLE FOR THE OTHER

"Does alimony still exist?" Mary Ellen wanted to know. We explained that over the years the term *alimony* had developed a negative connotation and was replaced by the less-charged term *maintenance*. Whatever it is called, it represents monetary support to the needy spouse. However, the concept of support that will last indefinitely, which was the general rule for wives under the pre-1980 law in New York, has fallen from favor. The eleven factors the court is directed to evaluate in deciding whether to award maintenance, and for how long and how much, emphasize the rehabilitative and temporary aspects, unless there is dependency.

In the past, the norm was for the woman to be the homemaker and the man the breadwinner. Today, when over half of the women between the ages of eighteen and sixty-two are working outside the home, the trend—not only in New York, but throughout the country—is to award lower spousal maintenance over a shorter period of time. And, of course, maintenance statutes no longer can be sexually discriminatory, as they were in New York before the Equitable Distribution Law; husbands can now sue for maintenance, although they rarely do. Mary Ellen was correct when she assumed that she needed to return to the job market, because the purpose of spousal maintenance for younger wives generally is considered to be rehabilitative in nature, not a lifetime annuity.

Simply stated, the court may limit support to the period that is necessary for Mary Ellen to become self-supporting at a level the court considers adequate. If Mary Ellen could not become capable of earning enough to meet her own financial needs, then the court might require her husband to pay maintenance permanently.

Temporary Support and Maintenance

Mary Ellen was understandably frightened when Jim reluctantly packed his bags and left. They had not yet made provisions for her financial support. She realized that this oversight was caused by the unusual circumstances of Jim's departure, but she feared being left without money for the duration of the divorce proceedings. She honestly had no idea how she would maintain the house and feed the two children and herself without Jim's paycheck safely deposited in their checking account.

Fortunately, the courts can intervene if one spouse is left with insufficient funds during the divorce proceedings. Temporary support during the divorce action is designed to maintain the status quo as nearly as possible while the divorce is pending. The court has discretion to consider some or none of the eleven statutory factors in setting temporary maintenance, pending trial. Your lawyer can obtain an Order to Show Cause and a subsequent Temporary Order, which will provide temporary payments until the final decree. Rarely will the temporary support be enough to maintain the former standard of living. Mary Ellen did not require an accountant's expertise to realize that Jim's income must now provide for two homes, their respective living expenses, and two lawyers. It was unlikely that she would receive as much for household expenses as she had been receiving prior to the separation. Courts will not impoverish the supporting spouse, or he simply may stop working. Rather, judges seek to leave both spouses with a fair share of the available resources to cover necessary living expenses.

FROM EACH ACCORDING TO HIS OR HER ABILITY

The husband's and wife's relative earning capacities and needs, the primary determinants of the term and amount of maintenance, are a function of many factors. Despite many advances in women's access to jobs in the past twenty years, women who work outside the home still tend to be in lower-paying job categories than men. Employed women with college degrees earn, on an average, less than the average for men with no more than an eighth-grade education. Mary Ellen had a college degree, but her work experience was limited, as were job opportunities in her particular field of teaching. Although educational level and work experience contribute to earning capacity, the courts will use discretion before assuming employability. A degree in history or a job as a clerk-typist fourteen years ago does not place one in high demand in today's job market. An award of spousal maintenance may be designed specifically to train the supported spouse for better employment through a return to college or a trade school.

Ability of the husband to pay necessarily limits the amount of support and even the possibility of providing support. To determine Jim's ability to pay, we looked at their tax returns for the last two years. Next we studied her accounts of their living expenses prior to separation. This helped establish the dollar needs of both parties. Only after deducting Jim's fixed expenses—rent, food, car, and medical—could we get an idea of what we might ask for support.

If your spouse's income comes from his or her privately owned business, you probably will need an accountant. Perhaps many private expenses are incurred by the business for tax purposes rather than being distributed as personal income. Of course, it is to the owner spouse's advantage to show a limited income. Obviously, the less income produced, the less money is available for spousal maintenance.

To Each According to His or Her Need

Longer marriages where the woman was the homemaker yield her relatively greater possibilities for permanent support. Besides having invested a number of years in her husband, the wife will be older and will likely have less current work experience. These last two factors limit her capacity to be self-supporting. A woman under forty is much more likely to find employment than is a woman over fifty. Whereas the younger woman may be awarded support and maintenance on a declining scale for a fixed period of time until she is employed and self-supporting, the older woman has a higher likelihood of being granted support until she remarries or receives social security.

The courts often consider the number and ages of the children involved. Perhaps it will be decided that it serves the best interests of the children for the mother to remain home rather than to find outside work. This often occurs when the wife has custody of children of preschool age. Nonetheless, over half of the mothers of preschoolers are in the job market.

If health is a primary issue in seeking spousal maintenance, be prepared to substantiate the claim. It may be necessary to support the spouse's claim of health problems with expert medical testimony. This, of course, would apply to either spouse, a wife who seeks support or a husband who claims that his ill health will reduce his future earning capacity.

Maintenance awards in New York divorce decrees are made in conjunction with property divisions. The courts consider the obligations and assets of both parties, including their separate property and the extent of marital property awarded to each spouse, when deciding about maintenance. The court, as well as the parties, is concerned about the total financial package.

With the court in each case applying the often conflicting statutory factors, there are no simple formulas adequate for predicting spousal maintenance. Our files contain many types of maintenance awards. The bottom line, of course, is individual circumstances. Wealthier clients may obtain $5,000 a month or more; other clients accept awards of $500 or less. Often maintenance payments decline in specified annual amounts on the theory that the dependent spouse should start becoming financially independent, but note that federal tax laws penalize maintenance reductions of more than $15,000 from one year to another during the first three years after maintenance begins.

AVOIDING SPOUSAL MAINTENANCE

It follows that the spouse wishing to avoid paying spousal maintenance will employ all of the factors that apply to need, but to his or her own advantage. For example, a husband may try to disprove need by establishing that his spouse has sufficient funds available to support herself. Perhaps he will attempt to prove that she is presently employable or will argue that she could liquidate the marital property she will receive and live off interest and dividend payments. If immediate quality employment is not possible, he may maintain that suitable training can be obtained in less time and for less expense than she claims is required. In this case he may need to employ experts in employment counseling to corroborate his claim.

If the financially stronger spouse cannot establish that the other can and should take care of herself financially, he may attempt to prove that he cannot pay what she does need. He may assert living expenses of his own that deny or sharply limit the funds available for support. He may point to factors that reduce or limit his future earning ability. Obviously the respective financial needs and abilities to pay of the spouses require careful investigation and balancing.

HEALTH INSURANCE

As Jim and Mary Ellen continue to try to establish themselves as individual economic and legal entities they will have to confront the problem of the availability of health insurance for themselves and their children. A divorce will not change the children's legal relationship to Jim—he will always be their father. Jim's medical insurance, available through his company, can therefore continue to provide coverage for himself and the children. Mary Ellen presents a different circumstance.

As long as Mary Ellen remains Jim's wife, separated or not, she probably will remain eligible to continue coverage as a member of Jim's family. Once a divorce is entered Mary Ellen no longer will be part of Jim's family and, most likely, Jim's insurance plan will provide that her coverage will terminate. Before 1986 this meant that Mary Ellen would have to seek out and secure health insurance without the benefit of any group rate. Depending on her medical condition and financial wherewithal, this could have disastrous consequences.

However, on July 1, 1986, a federal law went into effect known as COBRA (Title X of the Consolidated Omnibus Budget Reconciliation Act of 1985). This law applies to people who receive group health insurance and whose group has twenty or more people in it. The law requires that if a divorce would result in the loss of coverage, then the spouse whose coverage is terminated has the right to have an individual policy issued to him or her with the same level of coverage and at the group rate (plus up to 2 percent of the premium for administrative expenses).

Unfortunately, the law does not provide that you can keep this coverage forever. The best you can hope for is to keep the coverage for three years (less if the employer stops offering the insurance), and after that you are eligible for a "conversion plan," which does not have to offer the same level of benefits.

ATTORNEY FEES

There may be a question of responsibility for attorney fees. The law does not entitle either spouse to free litigation. A genuine need must exist before the law will require one spouse to pay the other's attorney fees. A disparity in income is not reason enough for the wealthier spouse to accept the responsibility. The award of attorney fees must be based on the honest financial need of one party and the ability of the other party to pay.

MAINTENANCE IN THE SETTLEMENT AGREEMENT

A well-drafted separation or settlement agreement guards against future problems and should help to eliminate the need for later modifiction. Therefore your attorney needs answers to the following questions before drafting your settlement agreement:

SPOUSAL MAINTENANCE CHECKLIST

1. If there are to be maintenance payments, are they fixed in amount or subject to fluctuation? How much do they decline in value? What factors cause fluctuation?
2. When are the support payments to be made? On what dates?
3. To whom are the support payments to be made? What are the penalties if they are late?
4. Can the spouse obtain income from employment or some other source without affecting the amount of the support allowance? If so, is there to be any limitation on the amount that can be earned?
5. When does the allowance to the spouse end?
6. How are the spouse's social security rights to be handled?
7. What are the tax consequences of the payments? If maintenance payments total more than $15,000 per

year there are rules under the Tax Reform Act of 1986 that must be carefully observed. If those rules are not followed, what are intended to be maintenance payments may become nondeductible to the paying spouse and nontaxable to the receiving spouse.

8. Are there to be security provisions, such as a bond, to guarantee the payments?

9. Who is to pay the parties' respective attorney's fees and costs of suit? How much? When?

10. Can the tax laws be properly applied to make attorney's fees legally deductible? Can the form of billing assist in a tax savings?

11. Who pays for audits, costs of transferring real estate, and other expenses incident to the dissolution of the marriage?

12. Is one party to pay the other party's attorney's fees and costs arising out of any postjudgment litigation? Under what terms and conditions is the party responsible?

13. Is cohabitation a reason for termination of support?

14. Is remarriage a reason for termination of support?

CHAPTER NINE

CHILD SUPPORT

PARENTS HAVE A LEGAL obligation to furnish financial support to their children in accordance with their abilities and circumstances. Until fairly recently a court, in setting child support, was required to consider various general criteria, such as the financial resources of the parents and the child, the health and emotional condition of the child, the child's vocational and educational needs and aptitudes, the standard of living that the child would have enjoyed had the marriage remained intact, tax consequences, and the nonmonetary contributions that the parents would make toward the care and well-being of the child. These criteria often led to inconsistant awards and seemed to invite parents to continually argue about the appropriate level of support.

On September 15, 1989, the New York Child Support Standards Act (CSSA) went into effect, providing for a certain standardization of child support obligations for families with a combined parental annual income of $80,000 or less. Where the family has more than a combined parental annual income of $80,000, a judge has broader discretion in making an award from the income above $80,000. This formula was designed to establish uniformity and reduce uncertainty. To a large degree it has done so. However, there remain some complications and unanswered questions.

WHAT IS INCOME?

Before the child support obligation can be established, the combined parental annual income must be determined. This amount is determined by adding the income of each parent. This is a concept that is easily understood on its surface, but clearly one-third of the CSSA is devoted to the definition of income.

Briefly, the law defines income as the amount that is or should have been reported as gross income on the most recent federal tax return (including wages and investment income, workmen's compensation, disability, unemployment, social security, VA benefits, pensions, fellowships, and annuities). The court also can add-in the value of certain "perks" and monies provided by friends or relatives. If the court finds that one parent has purposefully become unemployed or "underemployed," the court can attribute to that parent the amount of income he or she should be earning. Additionally, the self-employed parent will find that certain additions are made to his or her income to counter the effect of certain tax gimmicks.

Once income is determined, some deductions are authorized, including social security taxes, New York City income tax, and the City of Yonkers income tax.

DETERMINING THE PERCENTAGE

After each parent's income is determined, it is added together and then, assuming it is less than $80,000, the total income is multiplied by a percentage (17 percent for one child, 25 percent for two children, 29 percent for three children, 31 percent for four children, and no less than 35 percent for five or more children). Unfortunately, the law doesn't say which children are used to determine the percentage. If both parents have children only with each other and one parent has custody of all the children, the determination is easy. But what if the father has children from a previous relationship? What if the couple has three children, with the father having custody of one and the mother having custody of the other two? These questions are not clearly answered by the CSSA. As of this writing one appellate court dealt with the issue in a decision deciding three separate cases. One father had five children by two mothers now living in separate households, one had four children in three households, and one had four children in two households. Each father argued that the court should add the total number of children together, regardless of where they lived, and apportion the statutory child support among them equally. The appellate court rejected that method. Basically the court said that the support percentages are based on the financial requirements *per household* and reflect economies of scale. Consequently, the percentages should not be applied in a multiple household situation where the benefits of the economies of scale do not exist.

What is the answer? The CSSA provides that judges can depart from the guidelines if applying them reduces the paying parent's income below a certain amount or would be "unjust or inappropriate" under the circumstances.

DETERMINING SUPPORT

In an uncomplicated case the application of the CSSA is fairly straightforward. For example, John and Mary have three children. John earns $45,000 a year after deducting social security and city income taxes. John pays $5,000 a year in court-ordered maintenance to an ex-wife. Mary earns $12,000 a year after deducting social security and city income taxes.

John's income:	$45,000	
Less:	− 5,000—maintenance	
Net income:		$40,000
Mary's income:	$12,000	
Net income:		$12,000

Combined parental income:	$52,000
CSSA percentage (three children, one household)	× 29%

Basic child support obligation:	$15,080
John's share—77% ($40,000 ÷ $52,000)	$11,612
Mary's share—23% ($12,000 ÷ $52,000)	$ 3,468

In this example, if John has custody of the children, Mary will pay him $66.69 per week as child support. If Mary has custody, John must pay her $223.31 per week.

OTHER FACTORS

CHILD-CARE EXPENSES

If a custodial parent is working, receiving education, or training in order to work and incurs child-care expenses, the court must apportion these expenses between the parents. However, if the custodial parent is looking for work and incurs child-care expenses, the court may apportion the expenses.

HEALTH CARE

Health care expenses that are not covered by insurance must be apportioned between the parents, along with child support and child-care expenses. Unfortunately, no definition of the term *health care* is in the statute, and that will undoubtedly be a source of disputes.

EDUCATION

Under certain circumstances (such as where the parties can afford it, where the parents were educated in private schools or are college educated, or where a child has particular needs or talents) a court may order that private school, college, or special education expenses be apportioned. There is no requirement that these expenses be apportioned in the same percentage as the basic child support obligation.

DEPARTURES FROM THE GUIDELINE AMOUNTS

As we mentioned in the situation where there are multiple children in multiple households, a court has the ability to order child support in an amount that differs from the guideline percentage. The court can exercise this ability in the event that the combined parental income exceeds $80,000 or in the event that the court finds that the guideline amount would be "unjust or inappropriate." In determining whether it should depart from the guidelines, the court shall consider the following factors:

1. The financial resources of the custodial and noncustodial parent as well as those of the child;
2. The physical and emotional health of the child and his or her special needs and aptitudes;
3. The standard of living the child would have enjoyed had the marriage or household not been dissolved;
4. The tax consequences to the parties;
5. The nonmonetary contributions that the parents will make toward the care and well-being of the child;
6. The educational needs of either parent;
7. A determination that the gross income of one parent is substantially less than the other parent's gross income;
8. The needs of the other children the noncustodial par-

ent is supporting, provided that the resources available to support those other children are less than the resources available to support the children whom the court is dealing with;

9. Provided that the child is not receiving public assistance, the extraordinary expenses incurred by the noncustodial parent in exercising visitation or the expenses incurred by the noncustodial parent in extended visitation, provided that the custodial parent's expenses are substantially reduced as a result of the extended visitation; and

10. Any other factors the court determines are relevant in each case.

OPTING OUT

The adoption of the CSSA did not change the right of parents to freely enter into agreements concerning child support. Similarly, the adoption of the CSSA did not change the power of the court to oversee and, if needed for the benefit of the children, modify those agreements. There is certain required language that must be in your agreement in order to effectively render the CSSA inapplicable and still receive court approval. This wording should state that both parents are fully aware of the CSSA, what the child support would be if the CSSA were applied, and an explanation for why the CSSA is not being applied in your agreement.

MODIFICATION

Children grow, times and economic circumstances change. Parents find that in the latter stages of childhood it costs far more to raise a child than it did when the child was a preteen. In this regard the CSSA is disappointing by its failure to address these increases. According to the statute it costs just as much

(17 percent of parental income) to raise one two-year-old child as it does to raise a fifteen-year-old.

If a parent finds that the current level of support is inappropriate (that is, too much for the payor or too little for the recipient), a modification is possible. If the parents cannot agree and a trip to the courthouse is required, the court will expect the parent desiring the change to show a change in circumstances that is substantial and was unanticipated. Increases in support have been ordered where the parents' agreement was silent about paying the child's college expenses. But modification was denied where the only proof submitted was that the children were older and inflation had occurred. And a reduction in child support has been ordered where a parent suddenly became disabled and lost substantial amounts of income.

An interesting circumstance arises when the noncustodial parent remarries and has a child with the new spouse. In this event modification may be allowed, depending on whether the resources available to support the "new" child are less than the resources available to support the "old" child.

Support Checklist

1. How often and on what dates are the support payments to be made?
2. Are support payments reduced or waived in part during periods when the children are visiting with the noncustodial parent, when living away at school or at summer camp, or when the noncustodial parent contributes to day-care expenses? If so, by how much?
3. Are child support provisions to be designated as such in the separation agreement, or are they to be lumped together with the maintenance allowance for the spouse? (Tax consequences of this could be severe and should be discussed with the lawyer.)
4. Is there a specific amount allocated to each child?
5. Who claims which child as a dependent for income tax purposes? Under what terms and conditions will the

parent claim the children? What is the value of this exemption to each parent in after-tax dollars?

6. Are the payments to continue in whole or in part when the children become emancipated? Under what terms and conditions, and how?

7. Will support continue through college? Will it include college expenses?

8. Can the parent in charge of custody obtain income from employment or some other source without affecting the amount of child support he or she receives? If so, is there to be any limitation?

9. Is the custodial parent to receive any supplemental support for summer camp, religious training, music lessons, or other special expenses?

10. Who pays for the ordinary medical, dental, and optical expenses for the children?

11. Who pays for the extraordinary medical, dental, optical, and related expenses of the children? Which hospital, optical, orthodontia, dental, medical, surgical, counseling, or psychiatric expenses should be classified as extraordinary? Will this include family counseling expenses?

12. Is there any notice to be given to the noncustodial parent before extraordinary medical, dental, orthodontia, or optical expenses are incurred? If so, how much notice?

13. Who chooses the doctor, dentist, or other specialist?

14. Is medical insurance to be maintained? Who will pay for the insurance? What is the minimum extent of coverage to be provided? What evidence of coverage is to be given?

15. Are any medical, dental, optical, or related payments to be continued beyond the time a child reaches majority? Will it continue during the time a child attends trade school, college, or professional school?

16. Who pays the trade school or college tuition fees of the children? Who pays for graduate school, professional school, other special schooling?

17. Who decides what school, and the location of the

school, the children will attend? Who checks the ac-
creditation of the school?

18. What scholastic performance level must the children
maintain?

19. Is there a time limit by which the trade school or college
education, graduate school, or professional school
must be completed?

20. Who pays for room, board, fraternity or sorority,
money allowance, and other expenses incidental to the
children's education?

21. Who pays for travel expenses to and from school? Is
there any limit to the number of trips per school year?

22. Must children apply for loans, scholarships, or school
employment?

23. Must children carry a full academic program? Are grade
records to be made available to the noncustodial
parent?

24. Is there an effect on support if children have income
from employment?

25. May college expenses be paid directly to the children?

26. What is the effect of the child's dropping out of school
(leave of absence) and later returning? What about the
child's marrying before finishing school?

CHAPTER TEN

---※---

CHILD CUSTODY

NEW YORK law provides that neither the mother nor the father has a prima facie right to custody of the children. Both parents theoretically start as equals when they each ask a court for sole custody of their child. The court is to consider the best interests of the child and to award custody as "justice requires." The parent who is not awarded custody ordinarily will be given reasonable visitation rights.

Under present New York law the court seldom awards joint legal custody to parents who do not both agree that there should be joint custody. The theory is that if they can't agree that they want joint custody, they will not agree on the many decisions necessary for actually raising the child.

THE CHILDREN SHOULD NOT BE USED AS WEAPONS

Even though the children are not a proper subject for barter, sometimes they are used by either or both parents to obtain bargaining leverage. Each parent has a legally equal chance to win custody, although mothers usually get custody, particularly of younger children, as the mother usually has been the primary caregiver for the child before the marital breakdown. Even so, a threat to fight in court for sole custody may be used to obtain better financial terms for a husband who in actuality is ambivalent about wanting sole legal and physical responsibility for his children. He has something of value to give his wife, his legal right to seek custody, in exchange for something of perhaps great economic value to him. Conversely, if the wife has much the better chance of winning sole custody, should the court be forced to choose between the parties, the husband, who really wants agreed joint custody, may give up a lot financially to win his wife's agreement rather than risk losing a custody fight.

It is always a relief if and when a client says positively that there will be no custody battle. A fight between parents often takes a tragic emotional toll on all of the parties, particularly the children. With the diminished importance of marital fault in the divorce process, the litigation opportunities for spouses to express their negative feelings for each other have been narrowed. Where divorce litigation in New York once focused on what miserable and inhumane conduct by the other spouse justified granting a divorce, the focus today is on substantive issues: Who gets the house? What will the support payments be? Who gets the children? Thus, conflict over custody of the children can become a primary battleground between spouses who have not completed their psychological divorce.

MAKING THE CUSTODY DECISION

Before parents become embroiled in the custody issue, some serious questions must be answered. Do you really want sole custody? Will it serve your children's needs? Too often parents have a knee-jerk reaction about custody. Each seeks custody and endures a legal fight because it is socially expected, and they want to prove to the world how much they care about their children. Or, perhaps, a father lacking in parenting interests seeks custody out of spite, or because his ego has been bruised. Before plunging into a potentially destructive custody battle, consider your motives. Are you battling to protect your interest or those of your children?

The parents' decision should be prompted by the best interests of the children. Consider what you will have to offer your children, both emotionally and financially. What can your spouse offer? Can you cope with the demands of single parenting? How solid is your relationship with your children? What do your children want?

If the custody issue is left to the discretion of the court, the judge will assume the responsibility with great solemnity. The decision will be made according to his or her value system, not yours.

THE NEW YORK STANDARD

New York judges decide custody disputes based on the best interest of the child, and in doing so consider such factors as:

- the age and sex of the child
- the child's needs and the parent's situation and qualifications
- the number of children and their interrelationship (courts generally are reluctant to split up siblings without good reason, especially if they are young)
- the child's present adjustment to his or her home, school, and community
- the mental and physical health of all individuals involved
- the child's own preference, if the court finds that the child is of sufficient age and discretion

New York State's highest court has summarized our custody law as follows:

The only absolute in the law governing custody of children is that there are no absolutes. The Legislature has so declared in directing that custody be determined by the circumstances of the case and of the parties and the best interests of the child, but then adding "In all cases there shall be no *prima facie* right to the custody of the child in either parent."

Inform your lawyer of everything that you believe has a bearing on the custody choice. Tell your lawyer of any appointments your family has had with a social worker, psychiatrist, psychologist, or counselor. Also alert your lawyer if either you or your spouse has ever lost custody of a child before and under what circumstances this occurred.

THE CHILD'S PREFERENCE

It may be difficult to answer the question of whether the child truly prefers to live with you or with the other parent. In New York the preference of older children (at least eleven or twelve years of age) may be considered by the judge if custody is contested. Although judges are reluctant to permit children to testify, many will interview the child in private and may require expert testimony from psychologists or psychiatrists skilled in interviewing children. Judges realize that children often hesitate to make any comments for fear of alienating either parent.

The court, upon consent of the parties, will refer custody disputes to family counseling units maintained by the court to investigate custodial arrangements and make recommendations. The social worker will interview the parties directly involved as well as any physicians, psychologists, or other professionals whom these parties may have seen. The social worker also may choose to refer the child and the parents to professional personnel for diagnosis. The process may become a form of mediation for the parents in which they have meetings with the social worker and try to reach agreement on a custody and visitation scheme that works for them and their child. As mentioned in the divorce mediation chapter, California has had compulsory mediation for child custody disputes since 1981, and there have been proposals for similar legislation in New York. If the parents do not agree on custody during the counseling process, the social worker prepares a report with recommendations and sends it to the court.

WHICH PARENT IS MORE FIT?

After examining all of the reports the judge will make a decision concerning the fitness of the parents. The judge's guidelines include both emotional and physical health as well as the traditional moral fitness. Generally the court labels both parents as fit even though only one of the parents will be awarded custody. In theory the court should concern itself only with morality, including sexual morality, that truly affects a parent's relationship with the children.

Fathers' bids for sole custody of their children are no longer uncommon. A 1981 study found that 1.5 million single fathers were raising 3.5 million children. A landmark case involving Dr. Lee Salk, brother of Dr. Jonas Salk, of polio vaccine fame, was tried in New York in 1975 and changed the nature of paternal custody challenges nationally. Prior to that decision a father was encouraged to fight for his children only if he could prove the mother unfit. Traditionally the father's lawyer would pursue a line of questioning to establish extreme misconduct on the part of the mother—child abuse, alcoholism, prostitution. If negative behavior could not be attributed to the mother, the father was advised to forget about custody.

The Salk case took two years to resolve, but ultimately the father won custody of the children, aged two, six, and twelve, even though the court found that both parties loved the children and that both were fit parents. This case encouraged Jim in his custody effort. He was confident that any court would affirm both Mary Ellen and himself as fit parents but, like Dr. Salk, he hoped to prove himself to be the more fit parent.

Whether the court decides custody or the parents mediate and draft their own contract, the custody agreement is a matter of great importance. Generally the parent with legal custody has the right to determine the children's upbringing. This includes education, health care, and religious training as well as such day-to-day decisions as bedtime, enrichment programs, and visits to the doctor. In effect the custodial parent is given control of the children's lives, while the noncustodial parent's rights and responsibilities are limited to those listed in the decree. However, parents who are able to communicate with each other about the children may find it advantageous to agree to joint responsibilities for their upbringing. Joint custody agreements commonly name both parents responsible for education, summer plans, health care, and general welfare.

SEXUAL ABUSE CHARGES

Sexual and other abuse of children is more a part of life than we are comfortable acknowledging. Oprah Winfrey did a one-hour documentary in 1992 entitled *Scared Silent: Exposing and Ending Child Abuse* and stated at the beginning of the show that she had been sexually abused as a child.

In each of the shows's six case studies, the abuser, whether male or female, had been abused in his or her own childhood. Experts in the field have long known that patterns of child abuse tend to repeat themselves from generation to generation. Breaking the cycle often requires intervention by the police and courts as well as by mental health professionals.

Judges try to get children out of situations where they are being physically abused. If both parents have participated in serious abuse, the child may be taken away from the home and placed in foster care. If only one parent is guilty of abuse, sole custody generally will be given to the other parent and a court will impose restrictions on the abusing parent's access to the children. New York State has a hotline for reporting cases of suspected child abuse, and the reports are taken seriously.

The prevalence and seriousness of child abuse has led to another problem—false child abuse charges by an angry spouse immersed in a bitter divorce. An allegation that one has sexually abused a young child is a bit like being accused of being a Communist in Senator Joe McCarthy's heyday. The allegation itself can ruin you, and it is very difficult to disprove. Judges recognize the problem and are very harsh on a parent they believe has made a false abuse charge as part of his or her divorce tactics. Some judges believe that such cynical actions are inconsistent with being a fit parent and give sole custody to the other parent.

Even where there is good faith on all sides, finding the truth can be difficult. In one Texas case, a mother accused her estranged husband of sexually abusing their three-year-old daughter. The father vigorously denied it, but the mother sincerely believed that the abuse had happened. After court hearings it came out that the child had been abused, not by the father but by a teenage cousin on a rare visit to the mother's home.

Custody Modification

Custody decrees always remain subject to modification if the court finds that circumstances warrant this, although a court is naturally reluctant to disturb settled custody arrangements, particularly where the prior custody determination was made recently or after a full trial. Just what circumstances will justify a change in custody may vary from judge to judge. New York's highest court has stated that extraordinary circumstances are not necessary for a change in parental custody and that the best interest of the child should determine custody modification, just as they governed a court's initial custody determination. Custody modification will reflect the values and biases of the judge and the community, just as the original award did. The child's welfare depends in part on the continuity and stability of his home life, and the court will not change custody unless it finds that a change truly will benefit the child.

Some fact patterns encourage custody modification. One such situation is deliberate frustration or interference with the noncustodial parent's visitation rights. Additionally we have recently witnessed more and more situations that arise when a parent intends to move, perhaps as a result of economic oportunities elsewhere. The concept of "rehabilitative maintenance" compels the economically disadvantaged spouse to seek out, explore, and pursue job possibilities, and those may exist in areas far away from what was the marital home. In most cases this spouse is the woman, and if there were children, she is likely to have physical custody of them. Her need to take advantage of job possibilities and her desire to continue to have the custody of the children generally conflicts with the husband's desire to have easy and frequent access to his children. This problem requires the weighing of the different interests and an evaluation of what is in the best interests of the children.

People who are faced with this conflict have many paths available to resolve it. If the mother needs to move a substantial distance away from the father and if she is to retain custody of the children, the visitation schedule will likely have to be revised. Depending on the distances involved, the ages of the children, and the availability of transportation, the visits with the father will likely be less frequent but of greater duration. The new expenses of transporting the children will need to be apportioned between the parents. Often the noncustodial parent will have the children during most of the school recess periods and for an extended period during the summer months. Frequent telephone contact may be arranged. Like so many other matters, a negotiated solution to this problem can be designed to suit the needs and abilities of the parties involved. You, as parents, are generally best able to determine what is best for you and your children. If, however, you cannot reach an agreement, one of you will likely apply to the court for help. Trying to anticipate what the court will do is not easy, as every case is different.

The courts struggle to find a method for resolving these disputes and there are no hard and fast rules, nor any kind of formula, to predict accurately what a court will do in any particular circumstance. While courts have said that a parent needs to show "exceptional circumstances" to justify a long-distance relocation with children, the judges also have recognized that parents have a right to live the rest of their lives with reasonable freedom. The burden is placed on the parent who wants to move with the children to show that the move is necessary and that the children's best interests will not suffer. The provisions for maintaining contact with the non-moving parent are critical.

In the context of temporary long-distance relocation (say three months to a year), a recent decision held that a showing of exceptional circumstances was unnecessary, and the non-relocating parent would be required to show that he had a plan for the care of the child that provided more continuity in the child's life than if the child went with the moving spouse. As the child gets older, his or her wishes will be considered and the allocation of expense of long-distance visitation will be decided as well.

Another situation that calls for custody modification is child abuse or neglect. Any situation that threatens the child's physical or mental health will be viewed with concern by the court. This includes overt physical abuse and more subtle cases in which the parent consistently places his or her own interests well above those of the child—for example, cases where the custodial parent's lifestyle is inconsistent with important needs of the child.

Remarriage cannot, in itself, result in modification of the custody award. Most divorced parents do, in fact, remarry, and in many cases the child benefits from the new relationship with the stepparent. If, however, there arise within the new family difficulties that threaten the child's welfare, the court may modify the custody. For example, if the child and the stepparent are very hostile to each other, with little hope of improvement, or if the child's relationship with stepsiblings is so poor that it affects his or her emotional well-being, the court may change custody to the other parent. Modification should occur only if there is a change in the circumstances of the child or the custodial parent. A change in the circumstances of the noncustodial parent is rarely sufficient reason for modification.

Common sense tells us that sometimes the parents themselves find it necessary to modify custody. The courts recognize this need. If parents can reach agreement with each other in good faith, then, of course, they are the best judges of what is right for the children, and the courts will not interfere. However, a parent should never agree to a change of custody under coercion or threat from the other parent.

The Cold War: Violating the Decree

Even after the ordeal of hammering out an agreement and fighting for custody, there are parents who will continue the fight by violating the provisions of the decree. Violations range in severity. It may be only the custodial parent's failure, whether unconscious and innocent or deliberate, to have the children ready at the agreed time for the other's visit. Although that is aggravating, there are far more flagrant violations. Deliberate violations of the custody provision can make life miserable for both the children and the parents. Serious, ongoing violations may merit such disapproval that the court will change the custody arrangement entirely.

Too often parents use custody provisions to continue their war with each other. The visiting parent will repeatedly keep the children out late on the days spent together. The custodial parent will refuse visitation privileges because the monthly support check has not arrived. Besides being in violation of the decree, these tactics are clearly not in the children's best interests. Do not threaten your spouse with denial of rights given him or her in the custody decree. Besides being illegal, such threats may backfire and jeopardize your legal status with regard to your children.

What causes these infuriating violations? Perhaps the first action you should take is to examine your particular problem. You may be able to stop the violations if you determine that your own conduct is part of the problem. What is your reaction when the other parent consistently returns the children two hours late on visiting days? Do you rant and rave? It is entirely possible that your ex-spouse is playing a power game with you by deliberately flouting the visitation schedule in order to manipulate you and provoke conflict. If you respond in a low-key, emotionally relaxed manner instead of overreacting, he or she may realize that the manipulative tactic is not working and give it up.

If you cannot obtain the cooperation of the other parent in stopping violations, you should consult your attorney. The lawyers of both parties can then confer and perhaps reach a resolution of the situation. It is possible that your spouse's lawyer will be able to persuade him or her to cease the aggravating conduct. If not, you have the option of returning to court. Court-imposed remedies for custody violations will include an injunction ordering the offending parent to refrain from particular, specified conduct. Violations of the order can result in a finding of contempt, and in extreme cases, jail time can be imposed. Naturally it may be difficult to tailor a list of infringements precisely enough to completely cure the situation, and enforcement then becomes an additional problem.

CHILD SNATCHING

In the past, cases of parents "snatching" or kidnapping their own children and taking them out of the state have been a grave concern to families and courts. At the root of the problem was the willingness of different jurisdictions to reopen custody matters that originally were determined in other states. All fifty states have now adopted the Uniform Child Custody Jurisdiction Act, which was designed to discourage both child snatching and conflicts between states by giving deference to the first state's custody determination. The federal Parental Kidnapping Prevention Act of 1980 mandates that state courts honor (give "full faith and credit" to) existing custody decrees previously made by another state. That act also makes a federal criminal offense of parental kidnapping and also of interstate or international flight to avoid prosecution under child-snatching felony statutes.

One federal court's civil punishment of a father for child abduction produced a large monetary award to the custodial mother. After a scheduled summer visit with his two children, the father fled with them to Canada. When he was found, the mother sued for damages and the U.S. Court of Appeals affirmed the jury's decision to award the mother $130,000. The father and his relatives were found liable for that amount in compensatory and punitive damages for their abduction of the children.

In order to benefit from changes in the law, a parent must first know where the other parent has taken the children. The saddest of such cases involves the parent who has carried out his or her abduction plan in such secrecy that the other parent has no clue to their whereabouts. Unless information can be obtained from friends or relatives, the custodial parent may be helpless. Police and other law enforcement officials usually will not help beyond the borders of their own jurisdiction and, in any case, often are reluctant to be drawn into domestic matters. Thus, unless the parent can afford the services of a private detective, he or she faces a desperate situation without much hope, because the search can become a prohibitively expensive endeavor. The FBI's computers are now available to the search for missing children nationwide, a big help to parents of abducted children.

On July 1, 1988, the International Child Abduction Remedies Act went into effect in the United States. This act gave life to the Convention on the Civil Aspects of International Child Abduction, commonly called the Hague Convention. The Hague Convention is an international treaty designed to ensure that children who have been wrongfully removed from their home are returned promptly. The treaty applies to situations where a child is under sixteen years of age and has been removed from the possession of the rightful custodian, whether the right of custody be given by court order or by agreement. Many technicalities are involved in utilizing this treaty, and there are certain time limits which must be observed as well.

Once again, if you are facing this type of problem, a lawyer's advice is essential to determine your legal recourse. It is also urgent to act immediately. The longer your ex-spouse is gone with the children, the more difficult it will be to trace them.

Answering the following list of questions before the final decree will reduce the potential for future conflicts on custodial issues. Combine these questions with those following the visitation and joint custody chapters to guide you in developing a specific list for your own situation.

CUSTODY CHECKLIST

1. Which parent will make decisions governing the choice of schools, doctors, dentists, and surgeons? Is the other parent to be consulted?
2. Which parent is to make decisions concerning summer plans—camps, trips, and so forth? Is the other parent to be consulted?
3. Which parent is to make decisions in regard to religious training?
4. In the event of a dispute, is there to be arbitration or will you need to resort to a court for a decision?
5. May the children be permanently moved to another jurisdiction? Must the custodial parent first obtain permission from a court? Is there to be any notice to the noncustodial parent? How much notice should the noncustodial parent be given?

6. If the child is moved to another jurisdiction, how will the visitation provisions be adjusted?
7. Who will pay the transportation expenses for long-distance visitation?
8. What will be the frequency of telephone contact with the children? If telephone contact involves a long-distance fee, who will be responsible for the bill?
9. Is there to be any notice to the noncustodial parent in the event that a child becomes seriously ill or injured? Will the doctor be directed to make all information available to the other parent?
10. If the mother remarries, can the children's surname be changed to that of the stepfather? What remedies are open to the father?
11. Are the children to have any voice in any decision pertaining to their custody? At what age?

CHAPTER ELEVEN

JOINT CUSTODY

MANY DIVORCING parents are questioning the traditional sole custody system, where one parent has sole legal responsibility for the child while the other parent has visitation rights and obligations to pay support. Those parents want to *share*, after divorce, the problems, costs, privileges, and responsibilities of raising their children, more equally than is possible in the rigid "weekend daddy" formulas often set by courts. Such parents may opt for joint custody, also commonly described as shared custody or coparenting.

Shared custody often includes arrangements for the child to reside with each parent for alternating periods so that the child in effect has two homes. Shared *physical* custody is not essential, however, to the concept of shared *legal* custody. Critics of shared custody often focus on the logistical problems. It may, therefore, be advisable to separate the legal concept from its day-to-day reality in order to evaluate its merit.

THE LEGAL CONCEPT

At a minimum shared custody means that both parents have a legal responsibility for raising the child and making decisions about his or her education, health care, and general welfare.

It is a type of custody in which the parents need to maintain good contact with each other after divorce; they must co-operate to make joint decisions about the child's life. Clearly this will be effective only if the parents can, at least sometimes, calmly and reasonably communicate with each other. If it was not possible in the marriage, it may be unreasonable to assume it will happen after divorce. Symbolically and le-gally, under joint legal custody both parents have equal rights to raise the child. Neither is granted exclusive power to rear the child and neither is relegated to the position of visitor.

Joint physical custody includes joint legal custody and also means that the child lives alternately at each parent's home on a regular basis—for instance, one week at the father's house and the next week at the mother's house. The variations are endless, but the concept is that the child's time is split approximately equally between the parents and applies whether the child's moving cycle is twice a week or once a year.

Joint custody is gaining more acceptance for several rea-sons, but it seems to be a natural outgrowth of the broadening roles of men and women in our society. Married women no longer automatically stay at home to keep house and take primary responsibility for child rearing, as was the norm in the 1950s. At the same time, many men are assuming more responsibility at home. They actively seek to share in their children's lives, including the physical caretaking once con-sidered "women's work." Thus, the traditional sex-role ste-reotypes of housewife-mother and breadwinner-father are, to some extent, breaking down.

When such marriages head for divorce, parents naturally seek a custody arrangement reflecting these changing-role de-velopments. The father will not be satisfied with demotion to second-class status with his children, and the mother, with her outside job responsibilities, may not feel able to cope with the burden of single parenting. Shared custody can be a solution.

JOINT CUSTODY: IS IT FOR YOU?

Joint custody is not feasible in all cases. Here are some family characteristics that can contribute to the success of shared custody.

- Each parent should be capable of rearing the child.
- Both parents should accept frequent contact with each other. Especially in the early stages, shared custody involves communication. It requires real effort, cooperation, and frequent readjustment while working out unforeseen problems.
- Shared custody assumes that the parents have resolved the conflicts between them or at least have been able to subordinate them to a common concern for the child.
- Each parent sincerely wants active involvement in the child's life.
- The parents should live in reasonable proximity to each other if they are to share physical custody of the child with approximate equality. They need to live near enough to each other to make the residence changes practicable. Nearness extends to other considerations:
  - The age of the child—The younger the child, the less desirable it may be for him or her to move back and forth.
  - School arrangements—both parents should live close to the child's school.
  - Friendships—do other family members and close friends live nearby?
  - Financial resources—shifting between residences that are geographically far apart will be difficult if family finances are insufficient.
- Older children should favor a joint custody arrangement or at least not be opposed to it.
- Flexibility in the parents' jobs reduces conflicts. They need time off for the children's medical appointments and parent-teacher conferences. Parents without this flexibility can still make a joint physical custody arrangement

work, but it will be difficult. Parents who have committed themselves to shared physical custody rather than be content with weekend visitation often find that they must make sacrifices in their careers.

- Were the parents both actively involved in caring for the child during marriage? This is not an absolute prerequisite, but it clearly makes the transition easier for all concerned.
- Common goals for the children and similar attitudes toward child rearing are crucial. This is really a matter of shared values.
- Finally, do you have adequate financial resources? It is a mistake to assume that money alone is enough to make joint custody work, but it helps. Children need love and warmth, which money can't buy; they also need extra clothes if they shuttle frequently between Mom's house and Dad's house. A child may not have to have a separate room in each home to feel that he or she belongs, but having his or her own adequate space in both homes will help.

JOINT CUSTODY: THE PROS, THE CONS, THE UNKNOWNS

Joint custody remains controversial. Some experts warn that while it sounds nice in theory, it is often impractical in reality for two people split by divorce to agree on decisions concerning their children's welfare. In the name of efficiency, many lawyers therefore recommend the traditional sole custody award. To make an informed decision you should consider the advantages and disadvantages that are often discussed by experts in the custody area.

THE ADVANTAGES

Besides serving the goal of preserving the parent-child relationship, joint custody offers the following advantages:

1. The most important reason for joint custody is the minimization of psychological harm to the child. The mere fact of divorce probably will harm the child. But when one parent, in effect, divorces his or her children by giving up meaningful contact with them, the emotional damage is compounded. Most psychologists agree that the gravest harm to children of divorce is the loss of the relationship with one parent. If, as often happens, the noncustodial parent gradually fades from the child's life, the child usually perceives the absence as rejection by that parent. Consequently the child grows up with low self-esteem, a result of believing that he or she caused the problem and so is in some way unlovable. Of course, a particularly resilient child, or one with other strong familial support, can overcome the loss, but many, not so fortunate, do not. In cases where both parents are willing to make it work, joint custody may guarantee the ongoing role of each parent in the child's life, thus reducing the child's fears of losing either parent.

2. By dividing physical custody, the parent who would otherwise have sole custody has more time for his or her career and a personal life apart from the children.

3. The child will have fewer problems of divided loyalty in relation to the parents. Neither parent has been dubbed superior, and both have equal authority. Therefore the child is relieved of the considerable guilt often experienced by children in the traditional custody situation. When sole custody is awarded, children may feel resentment toward the custodial parent for having deprived them of the other parent. In addition, children may accuse the absent parent of desertion or may fantasize about the absent parent and yearn to live with him or her, thus engendering further guilt about the custodial parent.

4. Joint custody is inherently more flexible than sole custody awards. Because the parents have equal authority be-

fore the law, they can readjust custody arrangements as necessary when the family situation changes, without petitioning the court for modification.

5. Joint custody keeps the decision-making power with those who best know the needs of the children. It provides decision-making without interference by a court.

6. The effort required to make joint custody work provides excellent parental role models for the children. The child learns that love requires compromise and dedication to the interests of others.

7. Child support money may become less of a problem when both parents are participating actively in the care of the children. The need to transfer funds by monthly check may disappear as each parent assumes different support costs. At least the parents are likely to be more understanding of each other's needs when they share everyday concerns.

THE DISADVANTAGES

Joint custody has some inherent disadvantages. For example:

1. The joint custody arrangement may become an extension of the power struggle between parents who are unable to resolve their conflict.

2. The children may find it stressful to be shuttled back and forth between two households under joint physical custody. This argument is valid particularly for children under the age of seven or eight.

3. Joint physical custody restricts the mobility of parents because of the need for geographic proximity.

4. It may perpetuate the child's secret hopes for reconciliation of the parents.

5. Joint custody chosen for the wrong reasons may keep the parents from facing up to the reality of divorce.

6. Joint physical custody can be much more expensive because of the need to maintain two homes for the child.

LIVING ARRANGEMENTS: POTENTIALLY A MAJOR HURDLE

Working out residential arrangements can be a major problem. If the primary goal of shared custody is to preserve and strengthen both parent-child relationships, sharing physical care must be an integral part of the plan. Of course, the age of the child or the distance between residences must be considered. In most cases some sharing of physical custody is planned for. The big consideration lies in working out living arrangements that are not too burdensome or disruptive to the child's life.

In joint custody there can be a wide variety of residential patterns. In some families the child stays half the week with one parent, then goes to the other parent for the rest of the week. In other cases the child alternates residences weekly or monthly. There have even been cases in which the child lives for an entire year with one parent, then goes to the other parent for a year. Depending on the circumstances of those involved, each of these arrangements could be acceptable or otherwise, but they indicate the range of possibilities.

In a few families the children do not switch residences, the parents do. Thus, after each interval designated in the agreement, one parent leaves the central residence and the other parent comes in. Maintaining three households can be quite expensive. One suburban family manages a variation of this theme. The children reside in the "family" home. The parents share, on a rotating basis, an apartment in the city. Each parent spends two weeks with the children in the suburbs while the other parent lives in the city.

Clearly these arrangements would not appeal to all adults, but they may provide stability in the children's lives. They do show that great flexibility and imagination can be used in working out a satisfactory joint custody arrangement.

As mentioned previously, when children have two residences it is important that there be a sense of belonging at each place. Children should at least have their own corner, a place for toys and a few clothes, if not a separate bedroom. Most of all, children need to know that both parents want them and look forward to being with and caring for them, for that is the heart of joint custody or shared parenting after divorce.

It cannot be emphasized too much that a constant and sensitive awareness of the children's situation is a major responsibility for everyone—parents, lawyers, mediators, the courts—involved in a divorce action. Please read carefully the following Bill of Rights for Children of Divorce, prepared by the staff of the Family Court Counseling Service of Dane County, Wisconsin.

BILL OF RIGHTS FOR CHILDREN OF DIVORCE

1. The right to be treated as important human beings, with unique feelings, ideas, and desires, and not as a source of argument between parents.
2. The right to a continuing relationship with both parents and the freedom to receive love from and express love for both.
3. The right to express love and affection for each parent without having to stifle that love because of fear of disapproval by the other parent.
4. The right to know that their parents' decision to divorce is not their responsibility and that they will live with one parent and will visit the other parent.
5. The right to continuing care and guidance from both parents.
6. The right to honest answers to questions about the changing family relationships.
7. The right to know and appreciate what is good in each parent without one parent degrading the other.
8. The right to have a relaxed, secure relationship with both parents without being placed in a position to manipulate one parent against the other.
9. The right to have the custodial parent not undermine visitation by suggesting tempting alternatives or by threatening to withhold visitation as a punishment for the children's wrongdoing.
10. The right to be able to experience regular and consistent visitation, and the right to know the reason for a canceled visit.

CHAPTER TWELVE

VISITATION

DESPITE THE option of joint custody, most divorces leave one parent, usually the mother, with primary physical custody of the children. Visitation by the other parent is probably one of the least carefully considered provisions of most divorce agreements and decrees. This is unfortunate, because visitation can be one of the most frequent areas of postdivorce conflict. Visitation plans should be created to maintain the bonding between each parent and child. It can make the difference between a child who feels loved and secure and a child who feels the loss of one parent and lives in fear of losing the other.

Too often parents and their lawyers inappropriately fall back on the broad standard set by statute, which simply provides that the parent who does not have legal custody shall have "reasonable visitation." The divorcing parents are often so relieved to reach agreement in other areas that they are unwilling to delay the proceedings over visitation and assume that visitation will be worked out after the emotional friction has dissipated. But lawyers know that this friction sometimes does not dissipate and that visitation, as a remaining tie between parents after divorce, can become a new battlefield.

WORK OUT THE SPECIFICS OF VISITATION

In this working chapter, which has been designed to help you with the actual structuring of visitation, are sample visitation provisions for your consideration. Of course, you must use your own judgment in determining the visitation provisions you would like to have in your decree. In some cases conflict between the parents creates a need to account for every contingency. Other parents do not require much detail at all. But common sense tells us that a detailed agreement will help create a smooth transition in the initial stages of visitation. A provision merely for "reasonable visitation" invites disagreement as to interpretation.

Consider, for example, the case of Janet and Bruce, whose children were preschoolers when they divorced. The divorce left both parents with pain and bitterness. Janet got sole custody of the children by agreement. Then, with no real guidance, they simply agreed to reasonable visitation, with no further description.

As things worked out, Janet thwarted almost all of Bruce's attempts to see the children. She relied on the common excuse that the kids were sick or that seeing Bruce just did not fit into their schedule. She was still feeling hurt, and this was the only way she knew to inflict pain on Bruce. Consequently he did not see the children on a regular basis. After all, what is the definition of "reasonable visitation"? Bruce knew that any interaction with Janet created friction and further harm to the children, so he did not press his visitation rights. Instead he concentrated on establishing a new single life for himself.

Time passed and the wounds of divorce began to heal. The children were enrolled in school and Janet found herself working. Coping with single parenthood and work was often a burden. Janet now felt the need to share some of the responsibilities or, at least, to have an occasional weekend to herself. Bruce, however, was by now uncomfortable in the role of a parent. He had learned early in the divorce that his presence was not particularly welcome, so the new life he built for himself did not include parenting. The children really didn't know how to relate to him, although the son in particular wanted a close relationship with his father. Janet hoped that eventually Bruce would take the children on a regular basis, but so far this has not happened.

Recently their son John talked about his feelings: "When they got divorced I was only five and I really didn't know what was going on. But now I'm twelve and Mom treats me like the man of the house or something. It's a lot of pressure I don't need—and I can't handle it." He also spoke of his envy of other guys at school who could "do things" with their dads. Thus far there was no male replacement in sight, and he missed it. "Sometimes I get real mad I don't have a dad," he said. "But it's sad, too—how do I know it's not something I did that keeps him away?" John's fears are not unusual; as we have said before, many children feel that somehow they are to blame for their parents' divorce.

The custodial parent in this story could just as easily be the father, with roles reversed. Either way, the situation reveals some of the pitfalls of failing to plan adequately for visitation and then to follow the plan.

When parents begin to define agreed visitation they should be governed by the general welfare of the children. What are the children's specific needs? What is reasonable for them? Children of a divorce in the traditional custodial-noncustodial arrangement have two very general needs: a need for a consistent and loving relationship in a fixed single-parent home, and a need for ongoing contact and a loving relationship with the noncustodial parent. The New York courts have emphasized this factor of the child's need for a continuing relationship with the noncustodial parent. Parents who can manage to put the needs of their children ahead of their own bitterness are more likely to negotiate thorough and successful visitation plans.

RIGHTS OF GRANDPARENTS

While parents are considering visitation arrangements among themselves, they should be aware of, and possibly plan for, the desires and rights of grandparents to develop a relationship with their grandchildren.

For almost thirty years New York has recognized that grandparents may apply to the courts for visitation with a grandchild. The statute that governs this procedure originally applied only when either or both parents of the child were deceased. In 1975 it was amended to authorize such a request in other circumstances where "equity would see fit to intervene." When is it "fit for equity to intervene"? Basically when it would be in the child's best interest to do so.

Like so many other matters governed by the "best interest" test, grandparental visitation, to grant it or withhold it, is a decision that will rest in the sound discretion of the court. The cases that raise issues in this area are fairly few thus far and most involve a situation where the parents are divorced. Recently, however, the highest court in this state was confronted with two parents who were living together and both agreed that the child should not have contact with one of the grandparents. The court decided that the grandparent had an independent right to sue for visitation and was entitled to visitation if the grandparent could prove that a beneficial relationship with the child existed.

DEVELOPMENTAL STAGES OF CHILDHOOD

One wise strategy is to plan a mandatory annual review of the visitation plan to adjust it to the children's needs.

The children's specific needs change and redefine themselves as they develop through the different stages of childhood. Parents should be ready to adapt the visitation plan periodically to suit these various maturation stages. If a divorced family is flexible it can accommodate the changes on its own or with the help of a mediator. Rarely should it have to resort to the legal system.

Each child passes through six general developmental stages on the way to adulthood: infant, toddler, preschooler, early elementary, later elementary, and adolescent. An understanding of the needs of each developmental stage will help you design your own visitation plan. The following descriptions are by no means exhaustive, but they will serve to better identify these stages.

Infant (up to one year): The infant needs consistent physical care and the ability to develop and bond with at least one nurturing adult. From this consistency the infant will develop security. The infant child will have trouble dealing with long absences from the parent or parents to whom he or she has bonded closely.

Toddler (one to three and a half years): Toddlers continue the bonding relationship to the nurturing adult. They are learning to understand limits and to assert their own wishes against those of the parent.

Preschooler (three and a half to five): Children of this age are ready to expand the limits of their world. They may spend longer periods of time away from the nurturing adult. They achieve this expansion by developing relationships with other children in preschool, day care, or in the neighborhood.

Early elementary (five to nine): Children in elementary school are developing the ability to deal with their communities. Friendships with peers become more important. They are starting to develop a sense of ethics and of confidence in themselves as responsible individuals.

Later elementary (nine to twelve): Children of this age are becoming increasingly independent. They are taking more responsibility for matters that affect them. The peer group is of great importance.

Adolescence (twelve and older): Younger adolescents require more guidance than do older children. In this group, children need to be allowed to make decisions for themselves. Adolescents must be made to feel that their parents trust and respect them.

COMMON VISITATION SOLUTIONS

Divorcing parents who wish to go beyond the indefinite reasonable visitation provision commonly obtain provisions along the following lines in their decrees.

WEEKENDS

Times and dates should of course be varied to fit the needs of the child and the parents:

> Ordered, Adjudged, and Decreed that husband shall have visitation with the child on every other weekend, from Friday at 6:00 P.M. through Sunday at 6:00 P.M., commencing Friday, January_____, 19_____.

An alternative provision might provide:

> Ordered, Adjudged, and Decreed that husband shall have visitation with the child on the first, third, and, if applicable, fifth weekend of each month from 9:00 A.M. Saturday through 4:00 P.M. Sunday, commencing Saturday, January _____, 19_____.

HOLIDAYS

Parents must carefully consider how holidays are to be divided. Keep in mind the child's needs as well as your own. After all, how many turkey dinners can a child eat on Thanksgiving?

First list the national, local, religious, and school holidays. Holidays extending the weekend into three days should be considered when planning the normal alternate weekend visitation schedule. Though not considered legal holidays, Father's Day and Mother's Day, as well as the respective parent's birthdays, often are included in visitation schedules as well. Single-day holidays might be handled in this manner:

> Ordered, Adjudged, and Decreed that the father shall have visitation with the child on alternate legal holidays, Father's Day, and father's birthday. Holiday visitation will commence at 9:00 A.M. and continue until 7:00 P.M., except that if birthday visitation occurs during a school day this visitation will commence one-half hour after the child arrives home from school and continue until 9:00 P.M.

The parents may prefer to identify the specific holidays to be spent with the noncustodial parent. For example, they would substitute New Year's Day, Presidents' Day, and Labor Day for "alternate legal holidays."

If the parents determine that holiday visitation should be alternated yearly, inserting the words "in even-numbered years" will switch the holidays each year. The same principles apply to Jewish religious days.

EXTENDED VISITATION

It is particularly important that long-period visitations be handled well from the very first experience. Christmas, spring, and summer school vacations deserve careful planning. The noncustodial parent has the benefit of a longer visitation with the child and the burden of the longer-term responsibilities of caring for the children. This parent will be confronted with the day-to-day tasks and responsibilities assumed by the custodial parent, such as carpooling, day-care arrangements, enrichment activities, and an increased food budget. These temporary lifestyle changes require forethought and planning if the visitation experience is to be successful.

A broad provision covering Christmas and spring school recesses might provide:

Ordered, Adjudged, and Decreed that the father shall have visitation for a period of one week during the child's Christmas school vacation, the said week to begin at _____ o'clock _____.M. on the first day that school recesses and end at _____ o'clock _____.M. seven days later in odd-numbered years. In even-numbered years this visitation shall begin at _____ o'clock _____.M. on the eighth day before school reconvenes and end at _____ o'clock _____.M. on the day before school reconvenes.

This provision assumes that visitation is to be alternated yearly. If Christmas and spring visitations are to be for regular periods each year, then the reference to even- and odd-numbered years should be eliminated. If visitation occurs in the last half of a school vacation it is wise to allow the child to return home a day before school reconvenes. This gives the child some time to readjust before resuming school activities.

Christmas poses many problems for parents. Parents who celebrate Christmas want to share the package-opening experience with their children. This special event might be divided on the basis of Christmas Eve and Christmas Day as follows:

Ordered, Adjudged, and Decreed that the father (mother) will pick up the child at 9 A.M. on the 24th day of December of each year and return said child at 9 A.M. on the 25th day of December of each year.

The summer visitation usually lasts from two to eight weeks, depending on the age of the children, the distance to the noncustodial parent's residence, and the employment requirements of each parent. To permit both parents to plan their own summer schedules, a notice provision should be included. A typical provision provides:

Ordered, Adjudged, and Decreed that the father shall have the child for a period of fourteen consecutive days during the period of June through August, upon thirty days' written notice to the custodial parent. When the child attains ten years of age the summer visitation shall be increased to a period of twenty-one consecutive days, and to thirty consecutive days when the child attains the age of fourteen years.

CHECKLIST FOR A COMPREHENSIVE VISITATION PLAN

Comprehensive visitation plans include many provisions. You might want to consider all of the following in drafting your visitation schedule:

1. Include a clause specifying that the custodial parent will continue to reside in a particular geographical area.
2. Prepare a clause establishing provisions in the case that either parent moves away. This might require that the parents reach agreement on any move beforehand, and in case of failure to agree, that the issue shall be arbitrated.
3. Include a clause providing for free access between parent and child during times of illness.
4. Prepare a clause preserving specific visitation rights between the child and his or her grandparents.
5. Make provisions for the noncustodial parent to attend school conferences.
6. Include a clause that the noncustodial parent be made aware of the child's participation in recitals, demonstrations, and sporting events.
7. Include a clause stating that in the event of death or serious incapacitation of one parent, custody shall vest wholly in the other parent.

You may not wish to include all of these provisions, of course, but they indicate the way in which you should try to look to the future and anticipate possible problems.

MAKING YOUR VISITATION PLAN WORK

Once you have drafted a visitation agreement, you have to make it work. The change from being a live-in parent to being a visiting parent creates a new and very vulnerable relationship. If the child and the noncustodial parent have always shared a close bond, there will be additional pain beyond the emotional strains already created by the divorce.

With some foresight there are ways to minimize the burden of adjustment wherein you build a new relationship with your children. Effort should be made not to make the changes too rapidly. A "go-slow" pattern is especially crucial to the adjustment of very young children.

Each parent has the benefit of knowing far into the future when and where they will be seeing the child. The very young child has a different sense of time and may perceive an absence of a few days as abandonment. That child needs special attention during the transition to the new custody arrangement. If, for example, the noncustodial parent is to visit only on Saturdays it will be better for the parent to visit every evening for a while and gradually taper off to the weekend provision. Similarly, if your agreement allows you to take the child overnight it may be advisable to defer the overnights and begin with short, frequent visits to your new home. A very young child may be unnecessarily upset by being forced to spend the night in totally strange surroundings. Eventually the young child will be confident enough for regular extended visits there. But don't rush it.

It will help if your children have a place of their own at your new residence—somewhere for their own beds and belongings. This will reassure them that they have a permanent place in your new life.

If your children are older, you may wonder what to do on your first few visits. These may be awkward times for you, especially if you are not already close to your children. Some parents make the mistake of perceiving the visit as an occasion for mandatory entertainment. They expect, subconsciously or otherwise, that excursions to the zoo or sporting events help to compensate the child for what he or she has suffered during the divorce. This concept, frequently called the "Disneyland daddy" phenomenon, may lead the child to have an artificial view of the place in the child's life of the parent he or she is visiting, and it may undermine the establishment of a strong relationship between parent and child.

Children need fun time and work time with each of their parents. Avoid planning your visits only around "field trips." After all, you will have to talk sometime. Both of you need time free from distractions in which to examine your feelings about the divorce and get to know each other in a new way. We have repeatedly witnessed the great satisfaction that blossoms between the noncustodial parent and his or her child when the entertaining stops and they have the opportunity to discover a far stronger relationship. The relationship simply flourishes once they attempt to stay home, talk, and work together.

The presence of more than one child complicates conversation. If you have two children, you and your ex-spouse must consider whether each visit will include both children or will alternate, with each child visiting separately. This requires careful thought from both parents. You will need to consider the needs of the children and their relationship. If they do not get along well, this will be a factor in deciding how to arrange your visits.

Whether you have one or several children, you should recognize that once your visits are established it will be good for your child to invite a friend along occasionally. This will vary your experience together. It is also very important that your child's friends meet and get to know you. In so doing you will share more fully in each other's lives.

After settling into your visitation routine, you may find that the agreed-on weekly, or perhaps less frequent, visits are unsatisfactory to both you and your children. This is true particularly if you have had a close, happy relationship. This will be a lonesome time for all of you. You miss the children and they miss you. You will all benefit if you maintain contact in additional ways. Daily phone calls may be one answer. You may also want to write notes to the children and encourage them to write to you. Additional means of communication can go a long way toward easing the pain of separation. George Newman's book 101 *Ways To Be a Long Distance Super-Dad* is full of good ideas for maintaining communication in these circumstances.

VISITATION RULES FOR PLAYING FAIR

To help you and your spouse minimize difficulties in living with visitation, the following guidelines should be heeded.

NONCUSTODIAL PARENT

- If you have no prearranged schedule for visits, always give fair notice of an intended visit.
- Do not keep the children out too late; stick to the agreed-on hours.
- Do not make an appointment to see your child if you do not plan to keep it. Your child needs to be able to rely on you.
- If you must cancel a day visitation, give at least forty-eight hours' notice; give at least a week's notice for missing a multiple-day visitation.

BOTH PARENTS

- Do not use your child to spy on or carry messages to your ex-spouse; do not question the child about the other parent's activities.
- Do not belittle your ex-spouse to the child.
- Be willing to compromise on the timing of visits, especially as your child grows up, as your children have a right to a life and interests of their own.

CUSTODIAL PARENT

- Do not threaten to stop visits if child support checks do not arrive. The court cannot impose this sanction, and your interference with visitation could affect your custody status.
- Do not make excuses to block visits to the other parent. Your child has a right to see the other parent and needs both of you.

Remember, *visitation is a dual right*. It involves each parent's right to share in the life of the child and the child's right to know both parents and to enjoy their companionship. If you and your spouse remember your child's interests, visits will be happier and more beneficial for all.

CHAPTER THIRTEEN

COHABITATION AND ALTERNATIVE LIFESTYLES

MANY PEOPLE, including divorce survivors, are choosing to live together unmarried in close emotional, sexual, and economic relationships. Gays and lesbians do not have the option of bringing their relationships under the protective umbrella that marriage affords. Other couples, though heterosexual, consciously reject marriage for one reason or another. Living-together arrangements are different from marriages in that the state participates neither in the beginning nor in the ending of the relationship. There is no statute with special rules, like those the Equitable Distribution Law provides for married couples, to divide accumulated property once the relationship ends.

We limit our discussion of cohabitation to situations where one partner is economically dependent on the other during the relationship or where there is a pooling and sharing of resources. These relationships pose unique legal problems. Traditionally courts have not been very responsive when one party, often an economically dependent woman, asks for help when cohabitation ends. Sex outside of marriage violated state laws, and the state wanted to discourage cohabitation. But the law follows changing social, political, and economic realities, and cohabitation has arrived as a widely accepted lifestyle in New York and in other parts of the country.

152

This is why a chapter on unmarried cohabitation appears here, in a book about divorce. It has become such a common domestic arrangement that it demands recognition in a book on the severing of domestic arrangements. The Census Bureau tells us that in 1988 there were about two and one-half million unmarried-couple households, up from about one and one-half million such households in 1980. The bureau's definition of unmarried-couple households is "two unrelated adults of opposite sex who are sharing living quarters." The great majority of these households probably consist of "cohabitants" as we have defined them.

Even more striking than the fact that all unmarried-couple households increased more than fivefold from 1970 to 1988 is the fact that unmarried-couple households where the partners averaged between twenty-five and forty-four years of age increased sixteenfold, from about 100,000 in 1970 to about 1,600,000 in 1988.

In addition, the Census Bureau states that in 1983 there were about 750,000 households with only two unrelated male adults and about 500,000 households with only two unrelated female adults. It is difficult to estimate how many of those couples are gay cohabitants as defined above, but the figure is probably several hundred thousand.

LIVING TOGETHER: THE PROS AND THE CONS

Relationships are made more of feelings than of facts, so any decision to marry or live together should be based primarily on the feelings of each party. The legal protections of marriage are not needed by every heterosexual couple. However, no one should decide against marriage and for cohabitation without being well informed of the legal consequences.

Marriage laws protect the rights of parents regarding access to their children, the rights of children to support from the parents, and the rights of spouses to be compensated for their financial and emotional investment in their relationship. In addition married couples are given (1) preferential income, gift, and estate tax rates; (2) different social acceptance for themselves and their children; (3) insurance coverage for the death or injury of the other spouse; and (4) rights to the other party's estate, even if there is no will bequest, as well as to survivorship benefits from pensions and similar sources.

Living together may provide a couple more freedom and flexibility to craft a long-term relationship, particularly if one partner has a strong feeling against marriage, from experience or abstract conviction. Cohabiting may require more work than marriage, but some parties claim that it makes for a more exciting, vital relationship. Also, many couples use cohabitation as a trial period before marriage. We personally recommend to many clients who have gone through divorce that they try living with the new true love for a while before tying the knot. This is not illegal in New York, assuming that both parties are presently unmarried; however, if one party is still someone else's spouse, such a living-together arrangement is technically adultery, which is both a crime and a ground for divorce in New York.

An explicit, written living-together agreement is most appropriate where each party has good capacity to bargain with the other over personal and family needs. Relationships where one party consistently dominates the other are philosophically less suited for living-together agreements because the legitimate needs of the weaker party may not be stated or met, though much the same thing can be said for marriage. When parties have nearly equal bargaining strength, or where the party with greater strength uses it to create an agreement that works for both parties, the results can be quite satisfying. As one of our clients described it:

> It works because we're even and very careful. I've got an income, she's got an income, and we've both got property and the sort of respect that comes from knowing that each of us can go it alone if we have to. No kids though, as we agreed to get married if it came to kids.

Promise Me Anything, but Put It in Writing

New York, under the court of appeals 1980 decision in *Morone v. Morone*, 429 N.Y.S.2d 592, will enforce clear and definite oral or written agreements between cohabitants, *even though* the agreements give the cohabitants some economic rights and obligations similar to those the law gives to married couples. *Morone* involved an alleged oral contract to share the accumulated property. There are obvious difficulties in proving at a trial that there were conversations in which the parties agreed to divide property accumulated during cohabitation. It is the word of one against the other. Both cohabitants need the protection of a written agreement. A financially dependent cohabitant who takes care of the parties' home needs assurance that she will not be left penniless after years of being a homemaker. A wealthier cohabitant needs protection from exaggerated or fabricated claims for support or property division.

The *Morone* court says that New York has the power to enforce oral agreements in which the parties clearly agreed to divide assets accumulated during cohabitation or in which one cohabitant agreed to support the other financially. The deal cannot include compensation for sexual services the cohabitants supply each other. The *Morone* decision says that New York courts cannot infer a contract for property division or other compensation from the facts of a couple's living together like husband and wife.

Morone's rejecting the idea that cohabitants should get contract rights just from living together in a marriagelike relationship meant that Ms. Morone had to convince a court that Mr. Morone had made clear promises to her to share property in return for her domestic services. If she failed to prove such conversations with Mr. Morone, she would not get any of the property Mr. Morone had accumulated in his name (but through the couple's joint efforts), even though the Morones had lived together for twenty-three years and had produced and reared two children. Moreover, she could not qualify for support maintenance, which is reserved for spouses only under New York law. In New York, and perhaps all states, "palimony"—alimony for a nonmarried cohabitant—does not exist, because support and alimony rights are based on statutes that cover only spouses.

The wealthier partner also has uncertain rights and obligations under merely verbal contracts. How is an attorney to predict how successful a client's present heterosexual or gay lover may be in convincing a court, after the relationship has turned sour, that broad financial promises were exchanged in *conversations* during cohabitation? In that type of lawsuit the client probably will find that his version of the oral promises exchanged differs markedly from his ex-lover's.

At least four states, including California, under *Marvin v. Marvin*, 557 P.2d 106 (1976), do enforce implied contracts for division of property accumulated during cohabitation or for payment for services rendered. A court in California may therefore infer an enforceable contract from the conduct of an unmarried couple living together as if married. Whether a California court will infer a contract for a given couple, and what its terms will be, depends on the facts of the individual case, including the reasonable expectations of the parties. Michelle Marvin ended up without any recovery after the celebrated and prolonged *Marvin* litigation. The law constantly changes, and perhaps New York cohabitants will be able to prove and enforce contracts implied from cohabitation when and if *Morone* is extended. That possibility is another reason to put down in writing just what cohabitants expect of each other now and in the event the relationship ends.

SAFETY FIRST: ISSUES FOR A LIVING-TOGETHER AGREEMENT

Once the need for a cohabitation agreement is established, what should go into it? Basically, everything that the parties would want in a prenuptial agreement were they marrying instead of cohabiting should be included. The exception is that the written contract should not mention any sexual expectations the cohabitants have of each other. Not even New York or California, certainly among the more socially liberal states, will enforce a contract that is "meretricious" in Webster's sense of explicitly involving payment for sexual services.

Try to draft as much of the contract as you can on your own. Once you have done so, check with a lawyer who is experienced in this area. Like a medical exam, a small investment now could save you a much bigger one later.

Although each arrangement should reflect the unique needs of the parties, some elements may be common to most such agreements.

Separate property: What property will be held separately? How will it be managed in the event that the owner is incapacitated?

Common property: What portion will each party own of each shared property? How will purchase costs be shared? How will the payments, maintenance, and other responsibilities be shared? How will properties be divided if the relationship breaks down?

Separate income: What incomes will be considered separate? How will such income be managed by each party, and what will be done in the case that either party is temporarily or permanently incapacitated? Should each party give the other a strong power of attorney, allowing the other to conduct his or her affairs during incapacity?

Common income: What specific income or portions of income sources are to be shared? What living expenses and other uses will this shared income be used for, and how will such income be managed in the event that one party is disabled?

Modification, review, and termination of the agreement: How often will the agreement be updated, and how will it be modified? Will parties seek legal advice to insure that the modifications are valid? When and how can the agreement be terminated?

And for heterosexual couples:

Children: What will they be named? What provisions will
be made for their education? How will paternity be acknowledged? How will they be supported in the event of
a breakup or the disability of one of the parents?

Marriage: Will the agreement terminate if the parties decide to marry, or will portions of it carry over?

These are but a few of the concerns that should be addressed in a comprehensive living-together agreement. Each
couple has unique circumstances that create unique legal
problems that should also be addressed. The space limitations
of this book do not allow more elaboration at this point, but
this chapter plus your own research should allow you to put
together a basic agreement that you can then submit to a
lawyer for refinement. Remember that doing your own work
does more than save you legal fees. It provides you with more
confidence to manage your lives together and an agreement
that better reflects the uniqueness of your relationship.

STATUTORY COMMON-LAW MARRIAGE: NOT IN NEW YORK

Many states have statutes providing that couples who live
together and hold themselves out to the community as husband and wife have a legally binding common-law marriage,
even though there has never been a wedding. New York has
not had such a statute since 1933. However, common-law
marriage still exists in Alabama, Colorado, Washington, D.C.,
Georgia, Idaho, Iowa, Kansas, Montana, Ohio, Oklahoma,
Pennsylvania, Rhode Island, South Carolina, and Texas. If you
and your partner lived together in one of these states, check
with a lawyer to see if that state considers you married under
common law. If you are married under the laws of any state,
New York will recognize you as married here.

Your Property: How It Can Be Owned

Generally the law provides three basic forms of ownership that determine the disposition of property (in the absence of a contract) when the relationship breaks up. These are sole title, tenancy-in-common, and joint tenancy.

> *Sole title* ownership occurs when the title to the property is taken in one name only. When the relationship ends, the property will end up in the possession of the cohabitant whose name is on the title. Even if both cohabitants contributed to the property, either by purchasing it with joint funds or by providing services, the law sometimes will not protect the nontitleholder.
>
> *Tenancy-in-common* (or *cotenancy*) describes the situation where property is held by more than one person. Here, each person's name is on the title to the property and cohabitants would have an undivided one-half interest in property they own together. If one party dies, his or her half goes into his or her estate.
>
> *Joint tenancy* differs from tenancy-in-common in that it includes the right of survivorship. Thus, if one cohabitant dies, the surviving joint tenant or tenants get all of the property. If there are four joint tenants, the one who lives the longest would get everything.

Thus, tenenacy-in-common and joint tenancy are means of insuring that you will get your investment back when the relationship breaks up. Under either arrangement, each cohabitant can ask a court to divide the property and give each cohabitant his or her one-half interest. Sole title owners can convert to tenancy-in-common or joint tenancy, but this requires a conveyance of the sole owner's interest to both of them. This transaction can create tax consequences, so you should consult a lawyer before attempting it.

INHERITANCE AND YOUR PROPERTY

Persons who live together have no automatic rights of inheritance from their partner's estate. One solution is to make a will giving your cohabitant partner what you want him or her to have should you die. Particularly if you have significant properties, your will should be drafted and executed with care.

Mistakes and ambiguities invite conflict and court battles between your partner and your relatives, who may feel that living together does not create a strong claim to your money. If this happens and you have not made an adequate will, your relatives may succeed in preventing your partner's claim to any of the property you have shared. There is the example of one couple who had lived together and shared their earnings for forty years before one party died. Neither had written a will, so the surviving partner lost almost everything to his partner's family because title to all of their property was in his partner's name.

ABORTION, ADOPTION, AND PATERNITY

In January 1973, and again nineteen years later in June 1992, the U.S. Supreme Court held that the right of privacy included the right of a woman to decide whether or not to terminate her pregnancy before the fetus became viable. Thus it generally can be said that abortion is legal under certain circumstances and that the rules depend when it is done during the pregnancy. Each state has the ability to impose certain additional rules or regulations on women desiring abortions. The Supreme Court has stated that these rules or regulations will be invalidated if they create an "undue burden" on a woman's decision to terminate her pregnancy. The court has, however, held that physicians do not have to perform requested abortions. It is also the law that a father may not interfere with the mother's choice to abort. Minors, under certain circumstances, have the right to seek an abortion without their parents' consent. The "right to life" debate continues and is beyond the scope of this discussion. But whether and under what circumstances an abortion would be appropriate is an issue that some couples may wish to treat in their cohabitation agreement.

If abortion is not an option, adoption may be an answer if the cohabitants have an unwanted pregnancy. The legal procedure for adoption may be complex. Unlike abortion, the father may withhold his consent and thus bar the adoption. A 1972 U.S. Supreme Court decision held that the interest of a man "in the children he has sired and raised, undeniably warrants deference and . . . protection." As a consequence, New York has laws requiring that the father be notified of the intended adoption.

Parenthood without marriage creates even more, and somewhat different, problems than parenthood with marriage. The first concern is to legally establish paternity. The surest way is for the father to sign the birth certificate and to get a court declaration of paternity. You also will want to protect your child's rights in case you die. It is important for you to make adequate provision for your child in your will and to name him or her as a beneficiary for adequate insurance or other death benefits.

A child born to cohabitants is entitled to support from both parents, just as though the child had been born in lawful wedlock, and punishment for nonsupport is similar to that in the marriage situation.

Adoption by cohabitants, particularly gay cohabitants, can be difficult—perhaps more difficult than for a single parent. Some caseworkers who evaluate prospective adoptive parents regard cohabitants as less stable than single parents. The caseworkers fear that the child could be harmed by the breakup of the adoptive parents and, for heterosexual couples, question why the couple's commitment to each other has not led to marriage.

Living with Another During Divorce: The Risks

Most states make adultery a crime but rarely enforce the law. Except in pure no-fault states, adultery is a common ground for divorce. Moreover, in some states, if you openly live with a person awaiting a divorce you risk being sued for alienation of affections. New York, however, has done away with the alienation-of-affections cause of action. It is clear that persons not yet divorced who live together are, to some extent, compromising their divorce case, even though a criminal prosecution is extremely unlikely. Often the other spouse grows hostile and uncooperative when he or she discovers the cohabitation arrangement. That hostility could frustrate the entire divorce negotiation process.

Postdivorce custody and maintenance provisions can be affected by a cohabitation arrangement. New York statutes permit the modification of a prior court order awarding maintenance, if there is a living with and a holding out of another man as husband. Also, cohabitation may open questions of whether the parent's current living arrangement is suitable for children from his or her former marriage.

Changing Your Name: Changing Your Credit

Name changes can be granted to either cohabitant. The only statutory prohibition is that the change of name must not be designed to defraud. You need only go through a simple court procedure. By adopting your mate's name you may affect your credit rating; creditors may lump it together with that of your partner. Children born of unmarried parents historically were given their mother's surname. Now they may take the father's name as well. This can be accomplished by his written consent, by adoption, or by a paternity suit. Remember, however, that any of those options also gives the father significant rights, should the mother later wish to have the child adopted by a third person.

THE DILEMMA OF INSURANCE

Cohabitants have difficulty insuring each other, because most insurance companies require that the person buying the policy have an "insurable interest." Some insurance companies will not allow one cohabitant to insure the life of the other because they have no "interest" in each other. Moreover, it may be difficult for an umarried individual owning life insurance on his or her own life to name his or her cohabitant as a beneficiary upon death, because the class of persons you can name as beneficiaries also is limited by law.

Insurance companies can avoid their obligations by claiming fraud in the application. Thus, if you put down your cohabitant as your "wife" for beneficiary purposes the company can claim a breach of contract, alleging that they would have declined to issue the policy if they had known that the beneficiary was not legally your wife. You may have to shop long and hard to find a company that will insure you for the benefit of your cohabitant. Be certain that you are candid with the information you furnish the insurance company, lest you lose the entire policy.

The children of these relationships also have problems with insurance. In order to have an insurable interest in the life of their father, these children must show that he acknowledged them and that they relied on him to some extent for support.

Other kinds of insurance policies are also difficult for cohabitants to obtain. Although the usual homeowner's insurance policy has a clause that protects the other residents of the household, this usually is construed to mean members of the insured's family. The same is true of medical and hospitalization insurance. People who live together do not yet have the same "dependency" relationship, even though children certainly are dependent on their father! No legal spouse may well mean no insurance. As with life insurance, if you lie to get coverage for your cohabitant, you may lose your benefits.

SOCIAL SECURITY

One of the few legal benefits of cohabitation is social security. Senior singles who already have earned their social security benefits can live together and still collect two checks. If they marry the double payments end. A cohabitant cannot collect social security from a partner's account after the other's death. The children of these relationships, however, do derive benefits through both parents. Note that a deceased and unmarried worker father must be established officially as the child's father either by court order or by proven acknowledgment. In addition the worker must have been living with the child at the time of death or been contributing to his or her other support, and the child must have been entitled to inherit under the law of the state where they resided.

TAXES: THE EXTRA COST OF COHABITATION

Despite the "reform" amendments to the U.S. tax code during the 1980s, taxes remain a key source of confusion and anxiety for many people. This is true especially for cohabitants, because they are denied many benefits received by married couples in income, estate, and gift taxes. For example:

1. Cohabitants must file separate returns and may pay more taxes on their two individual returns than a married couple with the same income would pay on a joint return, particularly where only one party has significant income.
2. Any payment for companionship from one cohabitant

to the other could be taxed as "compensation for services."

3. Cohabitants must pay gift tax on major gifts given to each other. Gift tax is waived for gifts between married people.

4. Each cohabitant will be taxed for annual gifts to other persons over $10,000. A husband and wife may pool their exemptions so that one or the other may give $20,000 per year to a third party without having to pay a gift tax.

5. Upon death of a cohabitant, property passing from one cohabitant to the other is subject to estate tax. Upon death of a spouse, property passes to the other with significant estate tax exemptions.

6. When cohabitants end their relationship they may be subject to income and capital gains taxes for dividing their jointly owned property. When spouses divorce and divide their property they are less likely to be subject to income or capital gains taxes.

SPECIAL PROBLEMS OF GAY COUPLES

Although male homosexuals and lesbians remain largely outside the legal protections and opportunities that society gives to married couples, the times are changing. The concept of family continues to expand, and more people become included.

In the case of *Matter of Evan* (1992), a woman was allowed to adopt the child of another woman, thereby giving the child two legal parents of the same sex. The two women had been involved in a homosexual relationship for many years. They had lived together and raised the child together since he was born. The biological father had relinquished his rights to the child and the biological mother consented to her lover's adoption of the child. Presumably, should these women terminate their relationship, they will have to resolve issues of custody, support, and visitation, just like any other parents.

While the courts are liberalizing the concept of who can be a parent, the methods for achieving this status remain unchanged—you must be a biological parent or an officially adoptive parent. In order to be an adoptive parent one still must receive the consent of the biological parents or satisfy the requirements for dispensing with the consent. This concept was reaffirmed recently by the highest court in this state in denying parental rights to a biological mother's lesbian companion. In this case, like the *Matter of Evan*, the two women planned that one would bear a child, the child-rearing responsibilities would be shared, and the expenses would be shared. Everything went well for a while, with the child stating that he had two mothers. But the relationship between the women soured and they separated. During the initial period of the separation the nonparent continued to contribute to the expenses of the child and visited with the child on a regular basis. However, soon the visitation was halted, and she sued to reinstate it. As she was neither the biological nor the adoptive parent, her request was denied.

These cases are illustrative of the efforts people are making to get legal recognition for nontraditional parent-child relationships. As is often the case, the law changes after people do and so the pioneers are sometimes at a legal disadvantage, or at best in a legal limbo. This is evident particularly in the affairs of homosexuals, who, being denied the ability to marry, face the potential for a legal limbo that can be avoided only by formal agreements. Some of the areas that immediately come to mind are:

- Health care authority—who can tell the physicians what to do if the patient is incapable of communicating.
- Inheritance rights—with no will, there is no way.
- Succession to real property—no easy way to acquire title on the basis of the relationship.
- Health insurance as spouse or dependent—while certain inroads are being made, it is slow going.

Furthermore, tax benefits that are available to heterosexual couples are completely unavailable to homosexual couples, regardless of whether or not they have an agreement:

- Marital deduction for estate and gift tax.
- Deductability of support payments.
- Filing joint income tax returns.

LEGISLATION: A BETTER FUTURE FOR COHABITATION

Clearly cohabitants cross a minefield of legal problems. New York has solved some of these problems with *Morone* and other cases. Further change in this area, however, may require legislation. This legislation, from our viewpoint, should give adults who choose to form long-lasting cohabitation relationships, whether gay or heterosexual, and perhaps to raise children, protections and controls similar to those that New York now provides to married people. Such legislation must be very carefully drafted and create rules for cohabitant property analogous to those now provided for marital property. It is unlikely, however, that such legislation will be enacted in the near future.

Personally, we recognize and accept that many people believe that living together in a sexual relationship without marriage is morally wrong. Our position is simply that while people are free to make such moral judgments, the state should not abandon its concern for fairness and justice. We see no adequate reason why the housekeeping partner in a sensitive and productive long-term cohabitation relationship should not be given protections similar to those now received by the housekeeping partner in a long-term marriage. The argument that the housekeeping partner deliberately chose to live "a life of sin" and thus should be punished for that immoral conduct has little appeal when the practice has become so common.

APPENDIX A

---❖---

SAMPLE SEPARATION AGREEMENT

Note: The facts revealed in the following agreement were constructed by the authors and do not reflect an actual family.

AGREEMENT made this   day of August, 1992, between MARIA D'ANGELO, residing at 70-11 230th St., Unit 3F, Forest Hills, New York (hereinafter sometimes referred to as the "Wife" and/or "Mother," and/or "Maria"), and TONY D'ANGELO, residing at 88-11 3rd Drive, Rego Park, New York (hereinafter sometimes referred to as the "Husband" and/or "Father," and/or "Tony").

RECITALS:

A. WHEREAS, the parties were duly married to each other on June 11, 1982, at Roslyn, New York, before a chaplain in a non-denominational ceremony.

B. WHEREAS, there are two (2) children of the marriage, namely: Michelle Alicia, born August 16, 1985, and Rene Allyn, born January 19, 1987 (hereinafter sometimes referred to as the "Child" or the "Children").

C. WHEREAS, certain unhappy and irreconcilable differences have arisen between the parties, as a result of which they have separated and are now living separate and apart from each other; and

D. WHEREAS, the parties desire by this Agreement to confirm

their separation, to fix their respective financial and property rights, including the division of the parties' "marital property" as marital property is defined in Section 236, Part B of the New York Domestic Relations Law, to provide for the support of the Children, and to fix all their other rights, privileges and obligations and matters with respect to each other arising out of the marital relationship and otherwise; and

E. WHEREAS, the parties have each been fully, separately and independently advised of his or her legal rights, remedies, privileges and obligations arising out of the parties' marriage, by counsel of his or her choice, and each having been fully informed of the nature and extent of the property owned by either or both parties and of the income and prospects of the other party; and

F. WHEREAS, the parties each warrants and represents to the other that he or she fully understands all the rights and obligations he or she has under this Agreement, and each believes the Agreement to be fair, just and reasonable and to be in his or her individual best interests; and

NOW, THEREFORE, it is mutually agreed as follows:

ARTICLE I
SEPARATION AND NON-MOLESTATION

1.1 It is, and shall be, lawful for the parties at all times to live separate and apart from each other and to reside from time to time at such places as each may see fit and to contract, carry on and engage in any employment, business or trade which either may deem fit, free from control, restraint, or interference, direct or indirect, by the other in all respects as if they were single and unmarried.

1.2 Neither party shall in any way molest, disturb, trouble or interfere with the peace and comfort of the other or compel the other to associate, cohabit or dwell with him or her by any action or proceeding for restoration of conjugal rights or by any means whatsoever. Neither party shall directly or indirectly make statements to the other, or any other persons, which are derogatory of the other party.

ARTICLE II
CUSTODY AND VISITATION

Maria and Tony shall have Joint Legal Custody of the Children and the Children shall reside primarily with Maria, who shall have Physical Custody of the Children. Maria's rights as custodial parent shall be subject to the following provisions of this Article II:

A. Tony and Maria intend that Tony have meaningful access to the Children at all levels. All provisions of this Article II shall be interpreted consistently with this intention.

B. All major decisions concerning the Children shall be made by agreement between Tony and Maria. By "major," the parties mean (by way of example and not by way of limitation) decisions concerning: medical treatment, orthodontia, specialized training or lessons in matters academic, athletic or otherwise, summer camp, religious training and participation in various ceremonies (e.g., first communion and confirmation), marriage, post–high school education, employment, and involvement in activities that involve risk of bodily harm (e.g., contact football, automobile operation, scuba diving, etc.)

C. Tony and Maria also recognize that the Children will be living with Maria and nothing herein should be construed to limit Maria's right(s) to make and implement the day-to-day decisions of parenting (e.g., diet, curfew, attire, household chores, etc.). However, nothing herein should be construed to limit Maria's ability to solicit Tony's support, advice or comment in making or implementing the day-to-day decisions of parenting.

D. Maria and Tony hereby covenant to be reasonable in making decisions jointly and in deciding which decisions are subject to joint deliberation and which decisions are not. In the event of an impasse it is understood that Maria may decide the issue, although nothing herein shall be construed to limit the right of either party to apply to a Court of competent jurisdiction for review, reversal or any other appropriate relief concerning any matter governed by this Article II.

E. Tony and Maria agree that they will keep each other informed of the whereabouts of the Children and further agree that should any event or circumstance affect any of the Children's health or welfare, they will notify each other of such events or circumstances. Nothing herein shall be construed to deprive Maria or Tony of the ability to act unilaterally in the event of an emergency which directly affects any Child's well-being. Tony and Maria acknowledge that they are both responsible for the advancement of their children's health and their emotional and physical well-being. Tony and Maria acknowledge their responsibility to afford the Children their affection and give the Children a sense of security. Neither party shall, directly or indirectly, influence any of the Children so as to prejudice any of the Children against the other. Each party shall also endeavor to ensure that no third party (such as a grandparent, aunt, uncle, etc.) attempts to prejudice either of the Children against either Maria or Tony.

F. Nothing in this Agreement shall be construed so as to limit the presence of either Maria or Tony at any activity, event or function wherein any of the Children are participants and which occurs at a locale other than the home of either Maria or Tony. Tony and Maria agree that their respective attendance at activities, events or functions is desirable and Maria and Tony agree to give each other notice of all events, activities and functions wherein the Children are participants. Such notice shall be given as far in advance as possible.

G. Tony and Maria are entitled to complete, detailed and current information from any teacher, school or other entity providing instruction to any of the Children, and to be furnished with copies of all reports given by such teachers, schools or others. Maria and Tony each have the right to notify any such teacher, school or entity of his or her desire to receive such information. In addition Maria or Tony may request any school, teacher, or counselor of any and all conferences, sessions or meetings involving any Child and, in the event of such a conference, session or meeting, both Maria and Tony shall be entitled to attend and participate.

H. Each party has the right to communicate with any of the Children by telephone or otherwise, even though any of the Children are in the physical custody of the other. Such communication shall be only at reasonable hours and shall not interfere with the Children's meals, rest periods or schoolwork. Maria and Tony acknowledge that they will exercise restraint in calling the Children so as not to interfere with the other's time with the Children. Each party shall provide the other with current telephone numbers where any of the Children may be reached.

I. Each party shall be entitled to complete, detailed information from any school and other educational institution, any pediatrician, general physician, dentist, consultant or specialist attending the Child and to be furnished with copies of any reports available from them.

J. Each party covenants, represents and warrants not to cause the Children at any time to be known or identified or designated by any surname other than D'Angelo, and each party covenants, represents and warrants not to initiate or permit the designations of "Father" and/or "Mother" or their equivalents to be used by the Children with reference to a person other than the parties hereto.

K. Either party may remove the Children from the continental limits of the United States for vacation purposes for reasonable periods upon sixty (60) days' prior notice to the other parent together with a copy of the proposed itinerary of travel. In the event any common carrier, governmental agency (U.S. or foreign) or any other entity requires evidence of consent by Maria or Tony to either of them taking the Children from the continental limits of the United States, Tony or Maria shall execute any documents as may be required to evidence such consent.

L. In the event of a death of either Tony or Maria, the surviving party shall, forthwith, have the sole and exclusive jural and physical custody of the Children. In addition, the surviving parent(s) of Tony or Maria, as the case may be, shall, in the event of such death of either Maria or Tony, be granted meaningful access to the Children in order to preserve and foster any relationship they may have had with the Children prior to the death of either Maria or Tony.

M. The Wife shall not remove the residence of the Children from the counties of Nassau, Queens, Kings, Bronx, New York or the southern half of Westchester counties in the state of New York. If the Wife shall remove the residence of the Children beyond the above said limits without the consent of the Husband or permission of the Court, such failure shall be presumptive evidence of the right of the Husband to obtain physical custody of the Children and shall entitle the Husband to terminate further payments under this Agreement to the Wife for support and shall entitle the Husband to pursue any and all other lawful remedies. Nothing herein shall place any obligation on the Husband to give his consent to the Children's removal from the boundaries set forth herein.

ARTICLE III
VISITATION RIGHTS

Schedule of TONY'S visitation rights:

(a) Alternate weekends, commencing on Friday at 6:00 P.M. and terminating on Sunday at 6:00 P.M., unless the Friday or Monday adjoining that weekend is a federal holiday, in which event visitation shall expand to include said federal holiday.

(b) Four consecutive or nonconsecutive weeks (at Tony's election) during each school summer vacation period, provided that Tony gives notice to Maria of the weeks selected by him not later than April 15th of that year and provided that said visitation period will not interfere with the Children's summer camp or summer school, it being understood that the Husband and Wife will endeavor in good faith to arrange the summer visitation bearing in mind the requirements of Tony and the planned activities of the Children and of the Wife.

(c) On Father's Day each year from 9:00 A.M. to 6:00 P.M.; and on each Child's birthday for not less than three hours, said times to be arranged so that they will not interfere with the Child's education or other birthday activities; and the Husband's birthday for not less than three hours at such times when the Husband is not working, said times to be arranged in good faith so that they will not interfere with the Children's education.

(d) The first half of Thanksgiving, Christmas and Easter school vacation periods in odd-numbered years and the second half of said vacation periods during even-numbered years, except that visitation in Christmas vacation periods shall end or begin at 8:00 P.M. on Christmas Eve. The said vacation periods available for visitation shall commence at 6:00 P.M. on the last day of school which precedes the vacation period. If Tony should determine to exercise the foregoing rights of visitation for less than the entire period as set out in this paragraph, he may do so provided he gives Maria reasonable prior notice before commencement of the visitation period of the days which Tony has selected for the visitation and the same does not interfere with Maria's plans.

(e) Maria shall have the right to be with the Children during those portions of the above-named holidays and school recesses in which Tony has no visitation rights. There shall be no visitation exercised by Tony on Mother's Day.

(f) Such other or different times as the parties may hereafter agree upon.

ARTICLE IV
CHILD SUPPORT

4.1 Tony during his lifetime shall pay to Maria for the support and maintenance of the Children the sum of $963 per month (plus any increases or less any reductions as the case may be in accordance with the cost of living adjustment provisions set out in paragraph 2.2, below) on the first day of each month, commencing on the first month after the date hereof and continuing until the eldest Child is twenty-one (21) years of age (or sooner emancipated, as defined below). Upon the eldest Child reaching 21 years of age or sooner emancipation, the amounts payable by Tony to Maria will be reduced by fifty percent (50%). The monthly amount of child support set forth herein was determined by adding Tony's salary as a physical therapist of approximately $46,200 (after deducting New York City income and social security taxes) to Maria's earnings (after deducting New York City income and social security taxes) of $15,000 from selling Mary Kay cosmetics. That gave a total combined parental income of $61,200. This amount is multiplied by 25%, which is the child support percentage for couples with two children (resulting in $15,300 annual child support). This amount is prorated between Maria and Tony according to their respective incomes, Tony's share being 75.5% or $11,552—when divided by 12 equals $963.

4.2 As long as Tony is obligated to pay child support for the Children, the amount he shall pay will be annually increased or decreased, on the anniversary date of this agreement, by an amount which reflects the increase or decrease in the New York/

New Jersey region "All Producers Price Index" for the year preceding the particular anniversary. The support for the unemancipated Child[ren] shall be adjusted beginning August 1, 1993, and each August 1 thereafter ("anniversary date") to compensate for any increase or decrease in the cost of living from August 1, 1992, to the anniversary date.

The $963.00 monthly child support shall be adjusted on each anniversary date for each of the following months until the next anniversary date by a percentage equal to the percentage change in the Consumer Price Index—All Producers—New York and Eastern New Jersey ("CPI") between August 1, 1993 and the anniversary date. Should the CPI cease to be published, the parties shall use the index most commonly substituted for the same.

For example, if the CPI on August 1, 1993, is 5% above the CPI on August 1, 1992, the monthly payments shall increase to $1,011.15 for the month until the following anniversary date, subject to the other provisions of this Agreement. By way of further example, if the CPI on August 1, 1994, has fallen to 4% above the CPI on August 1, 1992, the monthly payments shall be $1,001.52 until the following anniversary date, subject to the other provisions of this Agreement.

4.3 All payments made by the Husband to the Wife under this Agreement shall be made by check or money order and forwarded to the Wife at her residence or at such other place for which she shall have given the Husband prior written notice.

4.4 Upon the happening of any event which shall result in the change or cessation of any payment to the Wife under this Agreement, said change or cessation shall be effective as of the next payment date following that event.

4.5 In addition to the other support provided in this Article, Tony will furnish at his own expense Blue Cross–Blue Shield insurance (or their equivalent) as is presently available to him through his employer, or by any subsequent employer, and major medical insurance as presently carried by him, for the benefit of the Children until their 21st birthdays, or emancipation as herein defined, and to share all unreimbursed medical expenses of the Children equally. "Medical expenses" shall mean necessary medical, dental, orthodontic and psychiatric expenses, prescription drug expenses and the cost of prescription eyeglasses. In the event that psychiatric expenses are excluded from future employer-provided insurance, such expenses shall be excluded from the definition of medical expenses herein.

4.6 Tony and Maria agree that they will promptly fill out, execute and deliver to each other all forms and provide all information in connection with any application either may make for reimbursement of medical, dental and drug expenses under any insurance policies which they may have. If either party shall have advanced monies for said expenses which are covered by insurance and for which a recovery is made for insurance claims filed for said expenses, the payment by the insurance carrier shall belong to the party so advancing said monies and any checks or drafts or proceeds thereof from the insurance carrier shall promptly be turned over to the party so advancing said monies.

4.7 Maria and Tony will furnish each other promptly upon the other's request documentation and other proof of their compliance with their obligation to provide health insurance coverage under this Agreement, and each party, in addition, is hereby authorized to obtain direct confirmation of compliance or noncompliance from any insurance carrier or employer of the other party.

4.8 The parties to the Agreement acknowledge that they have been advised of the provisions of the Child Support Standards Act (DRL Section 240 [1-b] and the Family Court Act (413[1]) (which are hereinafter collectively referred to as the "Act"). The parties understand that the Act sets forth guidelines based on percentage of income for the determination of the Husband's child support obligation, and they understand further that in the absence of this Agreement, the Act would govern. Each party acknowledges that his or her respective counsel has fully explained the probable impact of the Act were the rights and obligations of the parties to be determined thereunder and such explanations have been fully understood by each party. Notwithstanding such knowledge and understanding, the parties agree that all child support obligations between them be governed exclusively by this Agreement and they hereby waive application of the provisions of the Act.

ARTICLE V
SPOUSAL MAINTENANCE

5.1 Taking into consideration all relevants facts and circumstances, including but not limited to each party's employment and his or her employment potential, neither party seeks nor requires any maintenance or support from the other now or in the future. Therefore, no provision for the support of either party is made herein.

5.2 Each of the parties declares and acknowledges that he/she is possessed of sufficient income and assets to support himself/herself, and each hereby waives for all time any rights he/she may have or hereafter acquire to receive support or maintenance from the other. The parties each acknowledge that they believe this Agreement and, specifically, the release and waiver of maintenance or support to be entirely fair and reasonable.

ARTICLE VI
EQUITABLE DISTRIBUTION OF SEPARATE AND
MARITAL PROPERTY

6.1 In satisfaction of their respective rights to an equitable distribution of marital property pursuant to New York Domestic Relations Law, Section 236, Part B, the parties agree that their "marital property," their "separate property," as those terms are defined by said statute, and their marital debts shall be divided pursuant to this Article IV and Articles V and VIII.

6.2 Except as otherwise expressly set forth herein, each party shall own, as his or her separate property, free of any claim or right of the other, all of the items of property, real, personal and mixed, of any kind, nature or description and wheresoever situate, which are now in his or her name, control or possession, or which he or she is beneficially entitled to, or which may hereafter belong to, or come to him or her, with full power to dispose of the same as fully and effectually in all respects and for all purposes as if unmarried.

6.3 The Marital Residence

(a) The parties presently own as tenants by the entirety a condominium commonly known as 70-11 230th St., Unit 3F, Forest Hills, New York (the "premises"). Maria shall have the right of exclusive occupancy of the premises until the earliest happening of any of the following events: (a) the remarriage of Maria; or (b) the emancipation of both Children; or (c) Maria's removal of her permanent residence therefrom. Upon the earliest happening of any of the foregoing events, the premises shall be forthwith placed on the market for sale and sold as quickly as reasonably possible. The premises shall be available at reasonable times for inspection by brokers and by prospective purchasers. Both parties shall cooperate and use efforts reasonably calculated to produce the best sales price then available in the market and shall agree in a prior writing upon a gross offering price and a minimum net selling price. ("Net selling price" shall mean gross sales price less any broker's commissions.) If the parties fail to agree upon a net selling price, the same shall be determined as hereinafter set forth. Each party agrees to execute and perform a bona fide contract of sale to a disclosed third party principal which would yield an amount equal to or higher than the net selling price. If the parties do not agree upon a minimum net selling price, the same shall be fixed by an independent real estate appraiser designated by the then president of the condominium owners association/board of managers and the determination of that appraiser shall be shared equally by the parties. The appraiser shall ascertain the minimum net selling price by determining a value for which the premises can reasonably be expected to be sold in the then-present market and by subtracting seven percent (7%) therefrom, representing a broker's commission.

(b) Upon the sale of the premises, the net proceeds of sale shall be divided between the parties equally. "Net proceeds" shall be deemed to constitute gross receipts resulting from the sale of the premises less the usual expenses of sale. "Expenses of sale" shall be deemed to be any broker's commissions, transfer taxes, costs or fees imposed by the board of managers chargeable to the sellers, attorneys' fees for representation of each party on the sale, costs of satisfying the said existing first mortgage, agreed cost of repairs or allowance therefor to the purchaser in order to render the premises saleable or to perform the contract of sale, purchasers' financing or mortgage costs which are chargeable to the seller, advertising and other similar expenses incidental to the sale of the premises and the closing of title. Any moneys owed to the purchaser on account of the usual apportionments shall be paid for solely by Maria, and any moneys due from the same shall be her sole property. Division of "net proceeds" between the parties shall be made at title closing or as soon thereafter as practicable.

(c) Tony represents and warrants that all mortgage and tax payments in connection with the marital premises have been paid to date and that said first mortgage is not in default.

(d) Each party represents to the other that he or she has done nothing and will do nothing to encumber title to the premises except for the lien of the existing first mortgage.

(e) Until title closing, Maria shall be responsible for all expenses for the premises and its ordinary maintenance, including common charges, utilities, and repairs. Until title closing Tony shall make the monthly mortgage payment of principal, interest, insurance and tax escrows to 1st Nationwide Savings Bank. It is understood by both parties that the mortgage has a balance of $25,000 and that these payments by Tony do not constitute maintenance or alimony paid to Maria but are part and parcel of an equal division of the parties' marital property.

(f) Notwithstanding the foregoing, Tony shall be liable for one-half of the cost of any assessments imposed upon Maria by the condominium board of managers in order to pay for structural repairs required to be made to the premises or the common area of the condominium. Structural repairs shall be limited to repairs required by damage or deterioration (not caused or necessitated by acts or omissions of Maria, her guests or invitees or occupants of the house) to be made to footings and foundations and to replace the roof, exterior and supporting walls, boiler, electrical fuse panel, wiring and pipes (not damaged because of weather).

(g) Tony shall have the right, insofar as Maria is concerned, to claim income tax deductions for interest payments on the existing first mortgage and for realty tax payments. In the event Tony shall fail to make prompt payment of mortgage installments, insurance premiums and of realty taxes when due, Maria at her option shall have the right to make said payments on five (5) calendar days' written notice to Tony and to immediate reimbursement from Tony. Tony agrees to indemnify and hold Maria harmless of all loss, expenses (including reasonable attorneys' and accountants' fees) and damages in the event that he shall default in any of his obligations under this section of this Agreement.

6.4 The Savings Account

Tony and Maria have a savings account in Chemical Bank, Account #38754754644, with a balance as of the date of this agreement of $25,000.00. Simultaneously with the signing of this agreement, Maria shall pay to Tony the amount of $6,000, free of taxes, as part of a property settlement to Tony. Tony shall execute any necessary documents to convey the balance of the funds into Maria's sole name as her separate property.

6.5 The Automobile

Tony and Maria own a 1990 Toyota Camry automobile which they agree is worth $7,500. Tony shall, simultaneously with the signing of this Agreement, convey the automobile to Maria. Maria shall, from this date forward, pay the balance of $2,500 owned to GECC which sum is a lien against the automobile. Maria shall hold Tony harmless on this debt and, should she default in the payment of this debt, Tony may, at his option, pay the amounts outstanding and deduct such payments from any amounts owed by him to Maria under this Agreement.

6.6 The Furniture

Each party has furniture and furnishings in their possession at their respective residences and each party shall be entitled to keep these furnishings and furniture free and clear of the claims of the other.

6.7 Maria's Barbering License

During the marriage Maria studied at the NY Barbering School, applied for and received a license from the State of New York, #958-MJ-438743, to practice barbering. The parties recognize that this license enhances Maria's job prospects and earning capacity beyond that which she had at the time the parties were married.

In consideration of the promises made herein Tony hereby waives, relinquishes and releases any and all claims he has, had or may have in and to Maria's license or any future business or practice in which she may engage.

6.8 Tony's Physical Therapy License
Prior to the marriage Tony trained, applied for and received a license to practice physical therapy in New York. Maria acknowledges that this license is not marital property and that she has no claim to or right, title or interest in the license or any of Tony's future endeavors.

6.9 Maria's Inheritance
In 1990, Maria received the sum of $50,000 as her share of her grandfather's estate. The money was placed in a certificate of deposit in Citibank, account #23-09-87427. The parties agree that the $50,000 and all interest earned thereon is Maria's separate property and Tony waives and relinquishes any claim he may have thereto.

6.10 Credit Card Debts
Tony and Maria are jointly liable to Chemical Bank Visa for $5,700 and to Citibank MasterCard for $4,300. Tony shall assume, pay and hold Maria harmless upon these debts. Simultaneously with the execution of this Agreement, Maria shall give to Tony all credit cards in her possession concerning these two accounts. Maria shall incur no additional debts in these accounts.

6.11 Maria's IRA
Maria has a self-funded IRA at Chemical Bank in the amount of $7,500. Tony hereby waives and relinquishes any and all claims and rights which he may now have or ever acquire in the said IRA. Tony agrees that he will execute any spousal waivers as may be necessary, although this document may substitute for any other statement, prepared form or document that may be required by the Chemical Bank.

6.12 Tony's Pension Plan
Tony, through his employment at the Mt. Sinai Hospital, has a fully vested pension plan. The current value of the pension

plan, as determined by the ABC Actuarial Service, by agreement between Tony and Maria, is $75,000, all of which is marital property. The pension plan provides that a lump sum payment is available.

Maria shall receive a total of $15,000 from the Mt. Sinai Employee Pension Plan (SEPP) and the parties consent to the entry of a Qualified Domestic Relations Order (QDRO) as defined by Section 414(p) of the Internal Revenue Code of 1986 ("the code") and intend that said payment to Maria shall be made pursuant to the QDRO. Tony will, at his sole cost and expense, assemble all the information and necessary documents for a court of competent jurisdiction to enter a QDRO that will be approved by the administrator of SEPP.

ARTICLE VII
FINALITY OF EQUITABLE DISTRIBUTION

7.1 The parties intend this Agreement to constitute an agreement pursuant to New York Domestic Relations Law, Section 236, Part B. By this Agreement they intend to settle their rights and obligations to each other. Accordingly, except as otherwise provided, the parties mutually waive their rights and release each other from any claims for maintenance, distribution of marital property, distributive awards, special relief or claims regarding separate property or the increase in value thereof.

7.2 The parties intend that the real and personal property division, as provided in this Agreement, shall be final and irrevocable. Unless the parties execute a formal amendment to this Agreement, in writing, the separate property of a party shall remain such notwithstanding (a) a reconciliation of the parties; (b) rescission or termination of this Agreement.

7.3 Each party further acknowledges that he or she is accepting the provisions of this Agreement in full satisfaction of any claim to any property of the other party, whether owned individually or jointly or by any third party or parties, or whether separate or marital, he/she may have, have asserted or may ever assert, including any claim under Section 236, Part B, subdivision 5 of the Domestic Relations Law commonly known as the "Equitable Distribution Law," or any other applicable law of the United

States, the State of New York, or any other state, nation, territory or province now or hereafter having jurisdiction over the parties.

ARTICLE VIII
MUTUAL RELEASE AND DISCHARGE
OF GENERAL CLAIMS

8.1 Except as otherwise expressly set forth herein, each party hereby remises, releases and forever discharges the other from all causes of action, rights and demands whatsoever, in law or in equity, known or unknown, past, present or future, which each party ever had, or now or hereafter may have, against the other, including (without limitation) claims with respect to all separate property and all marital property as those terms are used in Domestic Relations Law, Section 236, Part B, or arising out of the marital relationship, except (1) any cause of action for divorce, annulment or separation, and any defenses thereto or (2) any cause of action arising out of or in connection with a breach of this Agreement.

8.2 Nothing herein shall be interpreted to prevent either party from suing for absolute divorce in any Court of competent jurisdiction and this Agreement shall not be deemed to condone or waive any claim which either of the parties may have against the other for divorce. This Agreement shall be incorporated by reference or otherwise in any decree that may be granted in any such divorce action, but shall not be merged therein and shall survive.

ARTICLE IX
RESPONSIBILITY FOR DEBTS

9.1 Except as otherwise expressly set forth herein, Maria represents and agrees that she has not heretofore, nor will she hereafter, incur or contract any debt, charge, obligation or liability whatsoever for which Tony is or may become liable. Maria agrees to indemnify and hold Tony harmless from all loss, expenses (including reasonable attorney's fees) and damages in connection with or arising out of a breach by Maria of her foregoing representation and agreement.

9.2 Except as otherwise expressly set forth herein, Tony represents and agrees that he has not heretofore, nor will he hereafter, incur or contract any debt, charge, obligation or liability whatsoever for which Maria is or may become liable. Tony agrees to indemnify against and hold Maria harmless from all loss, expenses (including reasonable attorney's fees) and damages in the event that a claim is made upon Maria in connection with or arising out of a breach by Tony of his foregoing representation and agreement.

ARTICLE X
ESTATE RIGHTS AND WAIVERS

10.1 Except as otherwise provided in this Agreement, each party hereby waives, releases and relinquishes any and all claims or rights he or she may have which exist or may hereafter arise by reason of the marriage between the parties hereto, with respect to any property, whether real, personal or mixed, belonging to the other party. Each party specifically, but not by way of limitation, waives and releases any and all rights that he or she may now have or may hereafter acquire, as a result of the marital relationship, under the laws of the State of New York or of any other jurisdiction to share in the other party's estate upon the latter's death, or to act as executor or administrator of the other party's estate upon the latter's death, or to participate in the administration thereof.

10.2 The foregoing waiver is intended to be and shall constitute a waiver by each party of (i) his or her right of election to take against any last will or codicil of the other, now or hereafter executed, under Section 5-1.1 of the Estates, Powers and Trusts Law of the State of New York, or any law amendatory thereof or supplemental thereto, or the same or similar law of any jurisdiction; (ii) any and all rights of setoff under Section 5-3.1 of such law, or any law amendatory thereof or supplemental thereto, or the same or similar law of any other jurisdiction; and (iii) any and all rights under Section 4-1.1 of such law, or any law amendatory thereof or supplemental thereto, or the same or similar law of any other jurisdiction, to receive any distributive share from the estate of the other in the event the other dies intestate.

ARTICLE XI
LIFE INSURANCE

11.1 Tony currently has $150,000 in life insurance provided to him by his employer. Tony shall maintain this insurance, with Maria as the primary beneficiary and the Children as secondary beneficiaries, in full force and effect until both Children are emancipated as defined below. However, when the elder Child attains 18 years of age, Tony may reduce the amount of insurance payable to Maria to the amount of $100,000, and may further reduce the amount payable to Maria to $50,000 when the younger Child attains the age of 18 years.

ARTICLE XII
INCOME TAX RETURNS

12.1 The parties shall file separate income tax returns unless they otherwise agree. Nothing herein shall impose a duty on either party to so agree. Tony shall be entitled to claim both Children as dependents on his tax returns from this date forward and Maria shall sign any documents required by any tax authorities in order to carry this provision into full force and effect.

12.2 If in connection with any joint federal, state or city income tax return heretofore or hereafter filed by the Husband and the Wife there is a deficiency assessment or a refund to be distributed, the amount ultimately determined to be due thereon or refunded thereon as the case may be, including penalties and interest, shall be divided between them based on which party's income, adjustments to income, deductions from income, credits against taxes or taxes already paid have resulted in the deficiency assessment or created the refund, as the case may be.

The parties agree that any dispute between them concerning this paragraph 12.2 shall be resolved by artibration under the rules of the American Arbitration Association, with the arbitrators having full powers to award attorney's fees, costs and disbursements to the prevailing party in such arbitration.

ARTICLE XIII
DEFAULT IN COMPLIANCE WITH THIS AGREEMENT

13.1 For the purposes of this Agreement, it is understood and agreed that in the event that either party shall institute a suit or other proceeding against the other party to enforce any of the terms, covenants or conditions of this Agreement and after the institution of such action or proceeding and before judgment is or can be entered, the defaulting party shall comply with such term or condition of the Agreement, then and in that event, the suit, motion or proceeding instituted shall be deemed to have resulted in a judgment, decree or order in favor of the party which began the suit or other proceeding.

13.2 Each party agrees that the other, in a single action or proceeding with respect to said payments and obligations, shall be entitled to sue for reasonable attorney's fees and disbursements.

ARTICLE XIV
LEGAL REPRESENTATION

14.1 Each party agrees to be responsible in full for his or her own counsel fees and disbursements with respect to all services rendered and disbursements incurred in the rendition of services in connection with the negotiation and consummation of this Agreement or otherwise and, in the event that the parties should be divorced, with respect to the rendition of all services up through and including the entry of a divorce judgment.

ARTICLE XV
FULL DISCLOSURE

15.1 Each party has made independent inquiry into the complete financial circumstances of the other and represents to the other that he or she is fully informed of the income, assets, property and financial prospects of the other, is aware of all separate property and all marital property as those terms are defined in Domestic Relations Law, Section 236, Part B, and is satisfied that full disclosure has been made, and that neither party can appropriately make a claim against the other by reason of failure to disclose or failure of knowledge of the financial circumstances of the other. Each has had a full opportunity and has consulted at length with his or her attorney regarding all of the circumstances hereof and acknowledges that this Agreement has not been the result of any fraud, duress or undue influence exercised by either party upon the other or by any other person or persons upon the other. Both parties acknowledge that this Agreement has been achieved after full disclosure, competent legal representation and honest negotiations.

ARTICLE XVI
WAIVER OF ADDITIONAL DISCOVERY

16.1 Maria further warrants and represents that she has been advised by counsel that she has the right and opportunity to take discovery in this matter by way of interrogatories, depositions and such other tools of discovery as may be available to her and that she has and does hereby waive her right to such discovery proceedings. Tony further warrants and represents that he has been advised by counsel that he has the right and opportunity to take discovery in this matter by way of interrogatories, depositions and such other tools of discovery as may be available to him and he has and does hereby agree to waive his right to such discovery proceedings.

ARTICLE XVII
EMANCIPATION EVENT

17.1 With respect to the Children, an emancipation event shall occur or be deemed to have occurred upon the earliest happening of any of the following:
(a) Reaching the age of twenty-one years;

(b) Marriage (even though such a marriage may be void or voidable and despite any annulment of it);

(c) Permanent residence away from Maria's residence. A residence at boarding school, camp or college is not to be deemed a residence away from Maria's residence and hence such a residence at boarding school, camp or college is not an emancipation event;

(d) Death;

(e) Entry into the Armed Forces of the United States;

(f) Engaging in full-time employment, except and provided that (i) engaging in part-time employment shall not be deemed an emancipation event; and (ii) engaging in full-time employment during vacation and summer periods shall not be deemed an emancipation event. Such an emancipation event shall be deemed terminated and nullified upon cessation, for any reason, from full-time employment.

ARTICLE XVIII
GENERAL PROVISIONS

18.1 This Agreement shall be construed and governed by the laws of the State of New York. This Agreement shall be a binding agreement upon the parties hereto, their respective heirs, executors, administrators, distributees, legal representatives and assigns.

18.2 In the event that any provisions of this Agreement shall be held illegal, unenforceable, or in conflict with the laws of the State of New York, such provision shall be deemed separable from the other parts hereof, and all of the other provisions shall be deemed separable from it, and all of the other provisions shall continue in full force and effect.

18.3 Each party shall from time to time hereafter execute and deliver forthwith any and all further instruments and assurances and perform any acts that the other party may reasonably request for the purpose of giving full force and effect to the provisions of this Agreement without any further consideration.

18.4 The failure of either party to insist in one or more instances upon the strict performance of any of the terms of this Agreement to be performed by the other party shall not be construed as a waiver or relinquishment for the future of any such term or terms, and the same shall continue in full force and effect. The terms of this Agreement may not be changed orally, but only by an agreement in writing signed and acknowledged by both parties, in the same manner as is required for the recording of a deed in New York.

18.5 Any and all notices or communications to be given by the Husband to the Wife shall be in writing and signed by the Husband and sent by him by mail to the Wife at 70-11 230th St., Unit 3F, Forest Hills, New York, or to such other address as she shall from time to time designate. Any and all notices or communications to be given by the Wife to the Husband shall be in writing and signed by the Wife and sent by her by mail to the Husband at 88-11 3rd Drive, Rego Park, New York, or to such other address as he shall from time to time designate. All notices shall be deemed given on the date mailed.

18.6 This Agreement may be executed by the separate signatures and acknowledgments of the parties hereto on counterpart copies thereof, each counterpart of which shall be deemed an original and of equal validity and effect with all of the others, and each of which shall be deemed a complete instrument when counterparts so executed and acknowledged have been exchanged by the parties.

18.7 The headings of the Articles and Recitals hereunder are for convenience only and shall not affect the meaning or construction of any provision of this Agreement.

18.8 This Agreement constitutes the entire understanding of the parties. There are no representations, promises, warranties, covenants or understandings other than those expressly set forth herein.

18.9 Each of the parties acknowledges that he or she is entering into this Agreement freely and voluntarily; that each of them has ascertained and weighed all of the facts and circumstances likely to influence their judgment herein, without duress of any kind; that each of them has been duly apprised of his or her respective legal rights; that all of the provisions hereof, as well as all related questions and implications, have been duly and satisfactorily explained to each of them; that each of them has given due consideration to such provisions and questions; that the Agreement is fair and reasonable; that each of them clearly understands and assents to all of the provisions thereof; and that each of the parties has read this Agreement prior to the signing thereof.

IN WITNESS WHEREOF, the parties have hereunto set their hands and seals the day and year first above written.

_____
MARIA D'ANGELO

_____
TONY D'ANGELO

ACKNOWLEDGMENT

STATE OF NEW YORK   )
                           : ss.:
COUNTY OF NEW YORK)
    On this   day of August, 1992, before me personally appeared MARIA D'ANGELO, to me known and known to me to be the individual described in and who executed the within instrument, and she acknowledged to me that she executed the same.

_____
Notary Public

ACKNOWLEDGMENT

STATE OF NEW YORK   )
                           : ss.:
COUNTY OF NEW YORK)
    On this   day of August, 1992, before me personally appeared TONY D'ANGELO, to me known and known to me to be the individual described in and who executed the within instrument, and he acknowledged to me that he executed the same.

_____
Notary Public

HISTORICAL AND POLICY OVERVIEW

from the 1987 Edition

BY HENRY H. FOSTER, JR., AND DR. DORIS JONAS FREED

THE CHAPTERS of *Divorce in New York* are confined to the specific issues involved in current New York divorces, and we consider it useful to explain briefly how New York divorce law became the way it is.

The original *judicial* ground for divorce in New York was adultery. In 1787 Alexander Hamilton, on behalf of a wealthy New York client, succeeded in obtaining the adoption of the adultery ground. Until September 1, 1967, adultery remained the only ground for divorce in New York, although most other states had long since adopted more expansive grounds for divorce.

The strict New York law of divorce imposed by religious and conservative groups led to "escape hatches" from the literal interpretation of the law. One was the bilateral divorce. In the nineteenth century New York began to recognize such divorces, obtained by New York residents in other states or foreign countries. The presence in person of one party in the other state's court and the appearance of the other at least by counsel was required. At the same time New York refused to recognize ex parte (or "mail order") divorces granted in other jurisdictions because the state wanted to protect the stay-at-home spouse (usually the wife) from the legal consequences of migratory divorce, including the loss of support.

Another escape hatch was an uncontested divorce at home in New York, which in this century became routine if the party charged with adultery did not bother to show up in court to defend his or her "honor." At the same time, commencing in the 1890s, annulment became a substitute for divorce, and alleged fraud was the most common basis for annulment. Statutes saved the legitimacy of children born of the annulled marriage; alimony and child support could be awarded on the same basis as in divorce cases. In many counties in New York the number of annulments far exceeded the number of divorces, and it was highly significant that, as in the case of divorce, nine out of ten annulment cases were uncontested.

Lawyers and judges had found ways to circumvent the strict divorce law on the books, and in actual practice the divorce process, not time in court, was where "the action was at." Negotiations in law offices dominated the picture. "Bargaining leverage" was crucial to the process.

The divorce process has become more and more focused on the rights of husband and wife to share in the joint or individual property of the couple. In 1980 New York made major changes in the division of property in a new law called the Equitable Distribution Law. The economic incidents of divorce before the Equitable Distribution Law help explain the dramatic reform of 1980.

First of all, the Divorce Reform Law of 1966, which became effective the following year, provided additional grounds for divorce in New York and eliminated the traditional defenses which were applicable only to the adultery ground. One of the new grounds was a no-fault ground in the sense that marital misconduct did not have to be proved where it was established that pursuant to written agreement the parties had lived separate and apart for a year or more. This really is "divorce by consent," because the parties, when they sign the agreement, know that a divorce may be readily obtained a year or more later by either party. Since 1967 the "separation" ground has become by far the most common ground for a New York divorce. It should be noted, however, that, off the record, the separation agreement may signify that there will be no contest if either party seeks a divorce on some other ground.

The Legislative Commission (which we assisted with research and drafting) had planned on rewriting New York alimony and marital property law as its next task on the agenda. It was urgent that a fresh look be taken at that area, because divorce had become easier in New York due to the new grounds and the elimination of defenses. The legislature, however, did not extend the life of the commission.

Independently in 1970 the authors of this overview started to research alimony and marital property law, and shortly thereafter the Matrimonial Law Committee of the New York County Lawyers Association, chaired by Julia Perles, Esq., made Professor Foster chairman of a subcommitteee to draft a proposed alimony and marital property law. Both the subcommittee and the committee worked for the remainder of the 1970s on what became the Equitable Distribution Law. There was frequent consultation with key members of the legislature and their counsel. The bill was first drafted in ideal terms; then changes were made in order to gain legislative acceptance. Bills passed in the assembly during four successive sessions, beginning in 1976. However, it was not until 1979 that favorable consideration was given by the Senate Judiciary Committee, after Senator Barclay had become its chairman. The measure probably would have passed in 1979 but for the belated opposition of a minority who demanded "equal" instead of "equitable" distribution. In June 1980 the legislature overwhelmingly rejected "equal" distribution and passed the Equitable Distribution Law, which became effective on July 19, 1980.

During this lengthy drive for enactment of the Equitable Distribution bill, minor changes or additions were made at the suggestion of an ad hoc committee of bar organizations, which had been enlisted to back and lobby for its passage. In addition, various legislators as well as counsel to the governor and for the Senate Judiciary Committee suggested minor changes or additions. Assemblyman Blumenthal and Assemblyman Burrows and his staff were most effective over the long haul in backing a bill that had a chance for passage. The remarkable thing, however, is that during its long incubation period the structure and substance of the Equitable Distribution Law remained intact, with its basic premise that modern marriage was an *economic* partnership, not merely a moral and social partnership. As a corollary to this new concept, the assets produced during the marriage by the efforts of one or both spouses, as well as the moneys spent, constitute the kitty to be equitably divided between the spouses upon divorce. This underlies the New York 1980 Equitable Distribution Statute. It sets a new public policy for New York.

What follows is a brief outline of New York law before and after July 19, 1980.

THE LAW BEFORE JULY 19, 1980 (THE EFFECTIVE DATE OF THE NEW EQUITABLE DISTRIBUTION LAW)

1. The only marital property distributable by the court between the parties was jointly owned property—for example, a home in the names of both parties or joint banking or savings accounts.
2. Property in the name of only one spouse was his or her separate property alone. All too often it would turn out that a devious or ungenerous spouse, usually the husband, had placed title to all assets accumulated during the marriage in his own name, and upon divorce the nontitled wife was entitled to none of the assets but was relegated to alimony alone.
3. Alimony could be awarded only to wives, not to husbands.
4. The primary duty to support wives and children was on the husband.
5. A wife found guilty of conduct that was grounds for divorce was barred from getting alimony.
6. Mothers usually were awarded child custody, fathers "reasonable" visitation rights.
7. No insurance coverage could be ordered by a court for the wife and family unless the husband agreed. If the husband dropped dead suddenly, alimony stopped and the wife and the family, without other resources, were often forced to resort to welfare.

THE LAW AFTER JULY 19, 1980 (THE EFFECTIVE DATE OF THE EQUITABLE DISTRIBUTION LAW)

1. The court must make an equitable distribution of all marital property when the marriage is terminated by divorce or annulment (not in case of a decree of judicial separation, which does not terminate the marriage).
2. "Marital property" is defined as all property accumu-

lated during the marriage by contributions or efforts of either or both parties.

3. "Separate property" is defined to include property owned separately by a party before marriage, property inherited or gifted by third parties, and compensation for personal injuries.

4. Legal title is irrelevant.

5. Property exchanged for separate property, as statutorily defined, retains that characteristic.

6. The appreciation in value of separate property is also separate property, except that if the appreciation in value is due in part to the contributions or efforts of the other party, that portion becomes marital property.

7. The parties may by formal written agreement designate what is marital property and what is separate property, before or during the marriage, and opt out of equitable distribution by the court. They can thus practically write their own ticket.

8. The guidelines set forth in the law must be considered by the court in making its equitable distribution, and the court must set forth in its decision the guidelines it considered and the reasons for its particular determination.

9. Among the most important factors is factor six, which requires the court to consider "any equitable claim to, interest in, or direct or indirect contribution made to the acquisition of such marital property by the party not having title, including joint efforts and expenditures and contributions and services as a spouse, parent, wage earner and homemaker, and to the career potential of the other party."

10. Where a division of particular property is impractical or burdensome, or where the distribution of any interest in a business, corporation, or profession would be contrary to law, in lieu of equitable distribution the court may make a "distributive award" to achieve equity between the parties. The distributive award may be payable by a lump sum or by installments, which, hopefully, will not be regarded as in the nature of taxable alimony.

11. Possession and occupancy of the marital home may be awarded, regardless of how title to the home is held; or title to the marital home and its contents may be transferred to one of the spouses alone.

12. The entitlement to maintenance is based on "reasonable needs" and ability to pay, and ten statutory factors must be considered in setting the amount and duration of maintenance. Again, the factors considered and the reasons for decision must be set forth in the opinion of the court.

13. Factor eight for maintenance repeats factor six for equitable distribution and requires that the court consider the nonmonetary contributions of a homemaker.

14. Maintenance is set for a particular period of time but may be extended if the recipient has not become self-supporting in the interim, or it may be modified upward or downward because of a substantial change in circumstances, including financial hardship.

15. Guidelines for child support are also set forth in the statute and child support is made a mutual obligation of parents, according to their respective incomes and resources, except that the nonmonetary contributions of the custodial parent to the care and well-being of the child must be considered in allocating the burden of child support.

16. The court may order that one party purchase, maintain, or assign an insurance policy covering health and hospital care and related services, to protect the other party and children; and the court may further order the maintenance of life insurance on the life of one ordered to pay child support or maintenance during the period of such obligation, with the other party or children named as irrevocable beneficiaries during that time.

17. Enforcement procedures for the collection of child support and maintenance have been tightened up by the New York Legislature.

18. Other services of the Domestic Relations Law have been made gender neutral (they apply to men as well as women).

The above outline constitutes the principal reforms achieved by the Equitable Distribution Law.

We believe that, for the most part, the law is being applied fairly by the New York courts. Unfortunately, there are some cases where in our opinion the law has been too narrowly construed, to the detriment of wives.

By far the most common complaint is from the women's groups who continue to demand equal rather than equitable distribution. Cases from other states, and New York cases as well, indicate in certain situations such a change would hurt more women than it would help. A wife of many years should be entitled to a greater proportion than 50 percent of the marital property, particularly where the husband has the ability to generate substantial new income. Moreover, the Equitable Distribution Law seeks to grant and maintain flexibility for determining what is fair and reasonable in individual cases. The contributions of some spouses are substantial, for others it may be minimal.

The proposed equal distribution presumption could become a rule of thumb that is applied inequitably and automatically. Is it not better to have the court weigh and balance the ten statutory factors and achieve a fair result? It is or it isn't, depending on your view of judges. It is interesting that in Pennsylvania women's groups wanted equitable distribution because they felt that they could get more that way from sympathetic judges, but in New York their sisters insist on equal distribution.

Finally, with regard to the agitation for equal distribution, would it not be arbitrary and often unfair to presume that a housewife is entitled to one-half the present value of the husband's business or professional practice? Obviously such an entitlement should depend on facts of the particular case, and the extent and value of the wife's contributions and efforts will vary considerably. The present statute, as is, provides the flexibility necessary to achieve equity under the facts of the individual case.

A 1986 amendment (Laws 1986, Chapter 844) to the Equitable Distribution Law restructured the factors for equitable distribution and for setting the amount and duration of maintenance. The most significant change in policy occasioned by the amendment was that the former emphasis on maintenance, based on reasonable needs and ability to pay, was shifted to "the standard of living of the parties established during the marriage." This change, obviously, was intended to raise the level of maintenance awards. The latter standard had been considered and rejected as idealistic and unworkable by the lawyers (of both sexes) who had drafted the 1980 statute. Their experience had shown that such an ideal might be achieved only where there was affluence or extreme poverty, because two households could not be maintained as cheaply as one. However, former factor six had listed standard of living during marriage as a factor to be considered "where practical and relevant." The 1986 amendment has no such limitations, and no distinction is made between short-term and long-term marriages or for cases where the parties lived beyond (or far below) their means.

Despite this significant change in policy, it is doubtful that courts will strip former husbands of what they are presumed to need to live in dignity and to continue to contribute support to the separated family. As previously mentioned in chapter seven on property division, three new factors were added for equitable distribution, each of which reflected prior New York decisions and appear to make no substantive revisions.

The new wording of the factors to be considered in setting the amount and duration of maintenance is another matter. Former factor three was changed to read: "The present and future earning capacity of both parties." This may become an entering wedge for an equalization of future income approach to maintenance that fails to distinguish between short- and long-term marriages and between dependent and self-supporting former wives.

Revised factor four now reads: "The ability of the party seeking maintenance to become self-supporting and, if applicable, the period of time and training necessary therefor." This appears to be a backhanded swipe at rehabilitative maintenance as distinguished from permanent maintenance, and to be an attempt to make the latter the norm.

New factor five for maintenance has no counterpart in prior law and reads: "Reduced or lost lifetime earning capacity of the party seeking maintenance as a result of having foregone or delayed education, training, employment, or career opportunities during the marriage." A literal application of this factor would be arbitrary and unjust in so many situations that it is apt to be ignored by the courts. No setoff is contemplated for what the spouse received in return during the marriage, and consideration is not given to who decided on a pure homemaker role, who gave grounds for or sought the divorce, and so forth.

Factor nine now reads: "The wasteful dissipation of marital property by either spouse." The term *family assets* was changed to "marital property." The reason for the change is not clear, but it may have been designed to give the nonbreadwinner greater control over the family pursestrings, as in community property states, where there is joint management of the community.

New factor ten now reads "Any transfer or encumbrance made in contemplation of a matrimonial action without fair consideration." This new factor is identical to new factor twelve for property distribution, and either restates prior decisional law, or is intended to make this factor considered twice, once for property distribution and again in determining maintenance.

New factor eleven is identical to former factor ten and reads: "Any other factor which the court shall expressly find to be just and proper." This is the catch-all provision designed to catch anything overlooked in the preceding enumerated factors. The other prior factors for maintenance are not changed by the 1986 amendment. Our conclusion is that the 1986 amendment was intended to better the lot of dependent spouses, but that in seeking that laudable goal the amendments may prove to be unfair or unworkable.

There is one practical way of reducing the flimflam that goes on in divorce cases and in law office negotiations. That is to remove marital fault from the Domestic Relations Law of New York. The fact that the marriage is dead, regardless of who killed it, should be sufficient for a legal interment. All states now have such divorce grounds—although in a few, as in New York, both parties must consent.

Although most matrimonial lawyers appreciate that no-fault divorce would be in the best interests of clients, children, and the public, and that marital fault grounds are counterproductive, some insist on the retention of the status quo, perhaps because they have a vested interest in things as they are. Bargaining leverage lurks in the background. The ability to hang the other party in limbo still exists in New York, although it may be a short-lived advantage if the party dangling in the breeze is free to move to an adjoining state. This bargaining leverage, which often is effective in the short run, ordinarily inures to the benefit of wives. Some female lawyers and feminists want to retain this bargaining leverage at all costs, and even some who formerly favored no-fault now campaign against it in order to retain bargaining leverage and unfair advantage.

It is not surprising, and it may be natural, for organized pressure groups and lobbies to seek to retain unnatural but accustomed advantages without regard to the best interests of children, the public, or themselves. The women's movement, notwithstanding the words of caution voiced by Betty Friedan, has valiantly fought sexual discrimination, but it also fights for special advantage and preferential treatment.

The welfare of children and of the public is overlooked when an issue becomes man against woman, woman against man. For example, men's groups have unsuccessfully opposed urgently needed federal and state reforms to improve the collection and enforcement of court alimony and support orders. They deserved to lose that one. But men's groups have attained a measure of success in pushing for a statutory preference for joint custody. They won in the New York Legislature, only to be thwarted by the success of the women's lobby in obtaining the governor's veto. Perhaps we need special pleaders for the interests of children and the public in order to offset the activity and to counter the propaganda of the active men's and women's groups. Unfortunately, such a proposed coalition would have difficulty in gaining the ear of public officials or the media, which already have taken sides on many issues that have other dimensions that are ignored.

New York divorce law changed and, we believe, improved greatly in the more than twenty years we have been closely involved with it. New York's Equitable Distribution Law is one of the most flexible and fair divorce statutes anywhere. New York still lags behind other states as it so far refuses to authorize true no-fault divorces, where either spouse can get a divorce just by telling a court that the marriage is over; but we are confident of progress on that front. We look foward to further improvements in a body of law that directly affects so many New Yorkers.

APPENDIX C

TEXT: NEW YORK STATE EQUITABLE DISTRIBUTION LAW

THE NEW YORK Equitable Distribution Law, Section 236B of the Domestic Relations Law, contains many of the basic rules discussed in this book. The text is constantly being interpreted and reinterpreted by New York State courts as they apply the law to specific divorce cases that do go to court. Therefore a lawyer's advice as to the current interpretations of the statute may be necessary to answer the specific questions in your divorce situation. The problem of interpretation has been further complicated due to the enactment of the 1986, 1989, and 1990 amendments to the Equitable Distribution Law of 1980. The text that follows is effective as of September 1, 1992:

Maintenance and distributive award.

1. Definitions. Whenever used in this part, the following terms shall have the respective meanings hereinafter set forth or indicated:
   a. The term "maintenance" shall mean payments provided for in a valid agreement between the parties or awarded by the court in accordance with the provisions of subdivision six of this part, to be paid at fixed intervals for a definite or indefinite period of time, but an award of maintenance shall terminate upon the death of either party or upon the recipient's valid or invalid marriage, or upon modification pursuant to paragraph (b) of subdivision nine of section two hundred thirty-six of this part or section two hundred forty-eight of this chapter.

b. The term "distributive award" shall mean payments provided for in a valid agreement between the parties or awarded by the court, in lieu of or to supplement, facilitate or effectuate the division or distribution of property where authorized in a matrimonial action, and payable either in a lump sum or over a period of time in fixed amounts. Distributive awards shall not include payments which are treated as ordinary income to the recipient under the provisions of the United States Internal Revenue Code.

c. The term "marital property" shall mean all property acquired by either or both spouses during the marriage and before the execution of a separation agreement or the commencement of a matrimonial action, regardless of the form in which title is held, except as otherwise provided in agreement pursuant to subdivision three of this part. Marital property shall not include separate property as hereinafter defined.

d. The term separate property shall mean:
   (1) property acquired before marriage or property acquired by bequest, devise, or descent, or gift from a party other than the spouse;
   (2) compensation for personal injuries;
   (3) property acquired in exchange for or the increase in value of separate property, except to the extent that such appreciation is due in part to the contributions or efforts of the other spouse;
   (4) property described as separate property by written agreement of the parties pursuant to subdivision three of this part.

e. The term "custodial parent" shall mean a parent to whom custody of a child or children is granted by a valid agreement between the parties or by an order or decree of a court.

f. The term "child support" shall mean a sum paid pursuant to court order or decree by either or both parents or pursuant to a valid agreement between the parties for care, maintenance and education of any unemancipated child under the age of twenty-one years.

2. Matrimonial actions. Except as provided in subdivision five of this part, the provisions of this part shall be applicable to actions for an annulment or dissolution of a marriage, for a divorce, for a separation, for a declaration of the nullity of a void marriage, for a declaration of the validity or nullity of a foreign judgment of divorce, for a declaration of the validity or nullity of a marriage, and to proceedings to obtain maintenance or a distribution of marital property following a foreign judgment of divorce, commenced on and after the effective date of this part. Any application which seeks a modification of a judgment, order or decree made in an action commenced prior to the effective date of this part shall be heard and determined in accordance with the provisions of part A of this section.

3. Agreement of the parties. An agreement by the parties, made before or during the marriage, shall be valid and enforceable in a matrimonial action if such agreement is in writing, subscribed by the parties, and acknowledged or proven in the manner required to entitle a deed to be recorded. Such an agreement may include (1) a contract to make a testamentary provision of any kind, or a waiver of any right to elect against the provisions of a will; (2) provision for the ownership, division or distribution of separate and marital property; (3) provision for the amount and duration of maintenance or other terms and conditions of the marriage relationship, subject to the provisions of section 5-311 of the general obligations law, and provided that such terms were fair and reasonable at the time of the making of the agreement and are not unconscionable at the time of entry of final judgment; and (4) provision for the custody, care, education and maintenance of any child of the parties, subject to the provisions of section two hundred forty of this chapter. Nothing in this subdivision shall be deemed to affect the validity of any agreement made prior to the effective date of this subdivision.

4. Compulsory financial disclosure. a. In all matrimonial actions and proceedings in which alimony, maintenance or support is in issue, there shall be compulsory disclosure by both parties of their respective financial states. No showing of special circumstances shall be required before such disclosure is ordered. A sworn statement of net worth shall be provided upon receipt of a notice in writing demanding the same, within twenty days after the receipt thereof. In the event said statement is not demanded, it shall be filed with the clerk of the court by each party, within ten days after the joinder of issue, in the court in which the proceeding is pending. As used in this part, the term "net worth" shall mean the amount by which total assets including income exceed total liabilities including fixed financial obligations. It shall include all income and assets of whatsoever kind and nature and wherever situated and shall include a list of all assets transferred in any manner during the preceding three years, or the length of the marriage, whichever is shorter; provided, however that transfers in the routine course of business which resulted in an exchange of assets of substantially equivalent value need not be specifically disclosed where such assets are otherwise identified in the statement of net worth. All such sworn statements of net worth shall be accompanied by a current and representative paycheck stub and the most recently filed state and federal income tax returns. Noncompliance shall be punishable by any or all of the penalties prescribed in section thirty-one hundred twenty-six of the civil practice law and rules, in examination before or during trial.

b. As soon as practicable after a matrimonial action has been commenced, the court shall set the date or dates the parties shall use for the valuation of each asset. The valuation date or dates may be anytime from the date of commencement of the action to the date of trial.

5. Disposition of property in certain matrimonial actions. a. Except where the parties have provided in an agreement for the disposition of their property pursuant to sub-

division three of this part, the court, in an action wherein all or part of the relief granted is divorce, or the dissolution, annulment or declaration of the nullity of a marriage, and in proceedings to obtain a distribution of marital property following a foreign judgment of divorce, shall determine the respective rights of the parties in their separate or marital property, and shall provide for the disposition thereof in the final judgment.

b. Separate property shall remain such.

c. Marital property shall be distributed equitably between the parties, considering the circumstances of the case and of the respective parties.

d. In determining an equitable disposition of property under paragraph c, the court shall consider:

   (1) the income and property of each party at the time of marriage, and at the time of the commencement of the action;

   (2) the duration of the marriage and the age and health of both parties;

   (3) the need of a custodial parent to occupy or own the marital residence and to use or own its household effects;

   (4) the loss of inheritance and pension rights upon dissolution of the marriage as of the date of dissolution;

   (5) any award of maintenance under subdivision six of this part;

   (6) any equitable claim to, interest in, or direct or indirect contribution made to the acquisition of such marital property by the party not having title, including joint efforts or expenditures and contributions and services as a spouse, parent, wage earner and homemaker, and to the career or career potential of the other party;

   (7) the liquid or non-liquid character of all marital property;

   (8) the probable future financial circumstances of each party;

   (9) the impossibility or difficulty of evaluating any

component asset or any interest in a business, corporation or profession, and the economic desirability of retaining such asset or interest intact and free from any claim or interference by the other party;

(10) the tax consequences to each party;

(11) the wasteful dissipation of assets by either spouse;

(12) any transfer or encumbrance made in contemplation of a matrimonial action without fair consideration;

(13) any other factor which the court shall expressly find to be just and proper.

e. In any action in which the court shall determine that an equitable distribution is appropriate but would be impractical or burdensome or where the distribution of an interest in a business, corporation or profession would be contrary to law, the court in lieu of such equitable distribution shall make a distributive award in order to achieve equity between the parties. The court in its discretion, also may make a distributive award to supplement, facilitate or effectuate a distribution of marital property.

f. In addition to the disposition of property as set forth above, the court may make such order regarding the use and occupancy of the marital home and its household effects as provided in section two hundred thirty-four of this chapter, without regard to the form of ownership of such property.

g. In any decision made pursuant to this subdivision, the court shall set forth the factors it considered and the reasons for its decision and such may not be waived by either party or counsel.

6. Maintenance. a. Except where the parties have entered into an agreement pursuant to subdivision three of this part providing for maintenance, in any matrimonial action the court may order temporary maintenance or maintenance in such amount as justice requires, having regard for the standard of living of the parties established during the marriage, whether the party in whose

favor maintenance is granted lacks sufficient property and income to provide for his or her reasonable needs and whether the other party has sufficient property or income to provide for the reasonable needs of the other and the circumstances of the case and of the respective parties. Such order shall be effective as of the date of the application therefor, and any retroactive amount of maintenance due shall be paid in one sum or periodic sums, as the court shall direct, taking into account any amount of temporary maintenance which has been paid. In determining the amount and duration of maintenance the court shall consider:

(1) the income and property of the respective parties including marital property distributed pursuant to subdivision five of this part;

(2) the duration of the marriage and the age and health of both parties;

(3) the present and future earning capacity of both parties;

(4) the ability of the party seeking maintenance to become self-supporting and, if applicable, the period of time and training necessary therefor;

(5) reduced or lost lifetime earning capacity of the party seeking maintenance as a result of having foregone or delayed education, training, employment, or career opportunities during the marriage;

(6) the presence of children of the marriage in the respective homes of the parties;

(7) the tax consequences to each party;

(8) contributions and services of the party seeking maintenance as a spouse, parent, wage earner and homemaker, and to the career or career potential of the other party;

(9) the wasteful dissipation of marital property by either spouse;

(10) any transfer or encumbrance made in contemplation of a matrimonial action without fair consideration; and

(11) any other factor which the court shall expressly find to be just and proper.

b. In any decision made pursuant to this subdivision, the court shall set forth the factors it considered and the reasons for its decision and such may not be waived by either party or counsel.

c. The court may award permanent maintenance, but an award of maintenance shall terminate upon the death of either party or upon the recipient's valid or invalid marriage, or upon modification pursuant to paragraph (b) of subdivision nine of section two hundred thirty-six of this part or section two hundred forty-eight of this chapter.

7.a. Child support. In any matrimonial action, or in an independent action for child support, the court as provided in section two hundred forty of this chapter shall order either or both parents to pay temporary child support or child support without requiring a showing of immediate or emergency need. The court shall make an order for temporary child support notwithstanding that information with respect to income and assets of either or both parents may be unavailable. Where such information is available, the court may make an order for temporary child support pursuant to section two hundred forty of this article. Such order shall be effective as of the date of the application therefor, and any retroactive amount of child support due shall be paid in one sum or periodic sums, as the court shall direct, taking into account any amount of temporary child support which has been paid. The court shall not consider the misconduct of either party but shall make its award for child support pursuant to section two hundred forty of this article.

b. Notwithstanding any other provision of law, any written application or motion to the court for the establishment of a child support obligation for persons not in receipt of aid to dependent children must contain either a request for child support enforcement services completed in the manner specified in section one hundred eleven-g of the social services

law; or a statement that the applicant has applied for
or is in receipt of such services; or a statement that
the applicant knows of the availability of such services and has declined them at this time. The court
shall provide a copy of any such request for child
support enforcement services to the support collection unit of the appropriate social services district
any time it directs payments to be made to such
support collection unit. Additionally, the copy of any
such request shall be accompanied by the name,
address and social security number of the parties;
the date and place of the parties' marriage; the name
and date of birth of the child or children; and the
name and address of the employers and income payors of the party from whom child support is sought.
Unless the party receiving child support has applied
for or is receiving such services, the court shall not
direct such payments to be made to the support
collection unit, as established in section one hundred eleven-h of the social services law.

8. Special relief in matrimonial actions. a. In any matrimonial
   action the court may order a party to purchase, maintain
   or assign a policy of insurance providing benefits for
   health and hospital care and related services for either
   spouse or children of the marriage not to exceed such
   period of time as such party shall be obligated to provide maintenance, child support or make payments of
   a distributive award. The court may also order a party
   to purchase, maintain or assign a policy of insurance on
   the life of either spouse, and to designate either spouse
   or children of the marriage as irrevocable beneficiaries
   during a period of time fixed by the court. The interest
   of the beneficiary shall cease upon the termination of
   such party's obligation to provide maintenance, child
   support or a distributive award, or when the beneficiary
   remarries or predeceases the insured.

   b. In any action where the court has ordered temporary
      maintenance, maintenance, distributive award or
      child support, the court may direct that a payment
      be made directly to the other spouse or a third per-

son for real and personal property and services furnished to the other spouse, or for the rental or mortgage amortization or interest payments, insurances, taxes, repairs or other carrying charges on premises occupied by the other spouse, or for both payments to the other spouse and to such third persons. Such direction may be made notwithstanding that the parties continue to reside in the same abode and notwithstanding that the court refuses to grant the relief requested by the other spouse.

c. Any order or judgment made as in this section provided may combine any amount payable to either spouse under this section with any amount payable to such spouse as child support or under section two hundred forty of this chapter.

9. Enforcement and modification of orders and judgments in matrimonial actions.

a. All orders or judgments entered in matrimonial actions shall be enforceable pursuant to section fifty-two hundred forty-one or fifty-two hundred forty-two of the civil practice law and rules, or in any other manner provided by law. The court may, and if a party shall fail or refuse to pay maintenance, distributive award or child support the court shall, upon notice and an opportunity to the defaulting party to be heard, require the party to furnish a surety, or the sequestering and sale of assets for the purpose of enforcing any award for maintenance, distributive award or child support and for the payment of reasonable and necessary attorney's fees and disbursements.

b. Upon application by either party, the court may annul or modify any prior order or judgment as to maintenance or child support, upon a showing of the recipient's inability to be self-supporting or a substantial change in circumstance or termination of child support awarded pursuant to section two hundred forty of this article, including financial hardship. Where, after the effective date of this part, a separation agreement remains in force no modification of a prior order or judgment incorporating the terms of said agreement shall be made as to maintenance without a showing of extreme hardship on either party, in which event the judgment or order as modified shall supersede the terms of the prior agreement and judgment for such period of time and under such circumstances as the court determines. Provided, however, that no modification or annulment shall reduce or annul any arrears of child support which have accrued prior to the date of application to annul or modify any prior order or judgment as to child support. The court shall not reduce or annul any arrears of maintenance which have been reduced to final judgment pursuant to section two hundred forty-four of this chapter. No other arrears of maintenance which have accrued prior to the making of such application shall be subject to modification or annulment unless the defaulting party shows good cause for failure to make application for relief from the judgment or order directing such payment prior to the accrual of such arrears and the facts and circumstances constituting good cause are set forth in a written memorandum of decision. Such modification may increase maintenance or child support nunc pro tunc as of the date of application based on newly discovered evidence. Any retroactive amount of maintenance, or child support due shall be paid in one sum or periodic sums, as the court directs, taking into account any temporary or partial payments which have been made. The provisions of this subdivision shall not apply to a separation agreement made prior to the effective date of this part.

c. Notwithstanding any other provision of law, any written application or motion to the court for the modification or enforcement of a child support or combined maintenance and child support order for persons not in receipt of aid to dependent children must contain either a request for child support enforcement services completed in the manner specified in section one hundred eleven-g of the social services law; or a statement that the applicant knows of the availability of such services and has declined them at this time. The court shall provide a copy of any such request for child support enforcement services to the support collection unit of the appropriate social services district any time it directs payments to be made to such support collection unit. Additionally, the copy of any such request shall be accompanied by the name, address and social security number of the parties; the date and place of the parties' marriage; the name and date of birth of the child or children; and the name and address of the employers and income payors of the party ordered to pay child support to the other party. Unless the party receiving child support or combined maintenance and child support has applied for or is receiving such services, the court shall not direct such payments to be made to the support collection unit, as established in section one hundred eleven-h of the social services law.

APPENDIX D

---◆---

PREPARING FINANCIAL INFORMATION FOR YOUR NEGOTIATIONS

Time is what a lawyer sells, and the more background work you do on your case, the less time you will need to buy from your lawyer. Your efforts to prepare your own background and financial information will save you money and make you a fuller participant in a process that is important for your future.

If you are doing your own divorce, you need to focus on what the financial needs and capacities of your new household will be. This checklist is intended to help you define the property and support issues you will need to settle with your spouse.

Even if you're using a lawyer, getting a firm grip on your financial situation gives you a sense of more control over what is happening to you. In fact, completing this difficult task as best you can is really an investment in the future—almost invariably, those who are actively involved at this point are better able to solve postdissolution problems without the aid of a lawyer.

THE BACKGROUND QUESTIONNAIRE

The aftermath of a divorce includes the creation of two households where one previously existed. That means that the same family incomes and resources may have to stretch to serve two homes. The information below is necesssary in order to assess the financial impact of the divorce on your future lifestyle.

Furnish this information for both spouses, not just yourself.

Unlike a medical history, a legal history involves three parties: you, your spouse, and the entity that you are about to dissolve, the marriage. You and your lawyer, if you have one, need to focus on the details, sometimes even intimate and embarrassing details, about all three entities to do a good job.

The following are blank questionnaires for your own use.

A. General Background

	Wife	Husband
1. Birthdate	_____	_____
a. Age now	_____	_____
b. Age when married	_____	_____
2. Date of marriage	_____	_____
a. Place (city)	_____	_____
b. County	_____	_____
c. State	_____	_____
3. Extent of education	_____	_____
4. Vocational skills	_____	_____
5. List when such skills last used	_____	_____
6. Religion	_____	_____
7. State all health problems since marriage	_____	_____
a. List doctors currently seen	_____	_____
b. List medications currently taken	_____	_____

B. Employment, Earnings

	Wife	Husband
1. Employer	_____	_____
a. Address	_____	_____
b. Telephone number	_____	_____
c. Job title	_____	_____

d. Length of
   employment   _____   _____
e. Work schedule   _____   _____
2. Information regarding family income from all sources
   a. List gross $_____ $_____
      income for past $_____ $_____
      three years (at- $_____ $_____
      tach copies of
      tax returns or, if
      unavailable,
      copies of W2
      forms)
   b. Present annual
      gross wage or
      income (attach
      pay stubs for
      last two pay
      months): $_____ $_____
   c. Other present
      and projected
      income, annual,
      including
      comissions,
      bonus, rentals,
      real estate
      contracts,
      pension, profit
      sharing,
      disability,
      unemployment
      or sick leave
      benefits,
      interest, public
      assistance, social
      security,
      dividends, and
      child support.
      Identify source   1) $_____   1) $_____
                         2) $_____   2) $_____

d. Projected
   annual
   gross income:
   total items 2.b.
   and 2.c.

	Total Gross	Total Gross
1990	$_____	$_____
1991	$_____	$_____
1992	$_____	$_____

e. Projected annual
   reductions from
   gross income
   (1) FICA SS   1) $_____   1) $_____
   (2) Federal,   2) _____   2) _____
       state and city
       income
       taxes (number of
       dependents)

Mother's Children from Prior Marriage

Name	Birthdate	Age	Present Custodian
(1)			
(2)			
(3)			

Father's Children from Prior Marriage

Name	Birthdate	Age	Present Custodian
(1)			
(2)			
(3)			

Are any children handicapped or disabled?   Yes   No
If yes, indicate which child and detail the problem.
Are any children adopted?   Yes   No
If yes, indicate if by stepparent or other.

LIVING EXPENSES: A MONTHLY BUDGET

Most of us have never made a budget, much less lived within one. However, the changes and uncertainties that the end of a marriage brings with it make budget planning just economic good sense. The hard facts of a divorce demand that you start planning your future living expenses now. You may want to consult a financial planner.

To prepare a monthly budget, start reviewing your check register or canceled checks. If you pay by cash or credit for most household expenses, start keeping receipts. Even if you pay by check you will be surprised at the number of items purchased with cash or credit, so do not forget to factor in these outlays too. The following form will help you prepare your budget.

In answering budgetary questions, calculate your expenses for the future, after separation. Take into account whether you or your spouse will have custody of the children. Calculate the children's expenses as if they will be living primarily with you, if that is a real possibility.

C. Monthly Expenses
1. Housing
   Rent, mortgage, and cooperative or
   condominium payments $_____
   Installment payments for improvements _____
   Installment payments for furniture and appliances _____
   Repairs, gardening, household help, miscellaneous _____
   Taxes and insurance (if not included in
   mortgage payments) _____
   Other: _____   _____
                         TOTAL HOUSING   _____
2. Utilities
   Heat (gas and oil) $_____
   Electricity   _____
   Water, sewer, garbage   _____
   Telephone   _____
   Other: _____   _____
                         TOTAL UTILITIES _____
3. Food and Supplies
   For _____ persons $_____

Supplies (paper, tobacco, pets)   _____

Meals eaten out   _____

TOTAL FOOD AND SUPPLIES $_____

4. Children

Baby-sitter $_____

Clothing   _____

Special health care or treatment not
  included in paragraph six, below   _____

Lessons, sports, clubs, camp   _____

School expenses (not tuition)   _____

Tuition (if any)   _____

Haircuts, personal expenses, allowances   _____

TOTAL EXPENSES OF CHILDREN   _____

5. Transportation

Vehicle payments or leases $_____

Vehicle insurance and license   _____

Vehicle gas, oil, ordinary maintenance   _____

Vehicle repairs (identify)   _____

Parking, tolls   _____

Taxi or public transportation   _____

TOTAL TRANSPORTATION   _____

6. Health care (omit if fully covered)

Insurance $_____

Uninsured dental expense   _____

Uninsured medical expense   _____

Uninsured eye care expense   _____

Uninsured drugs, prosthetics, and so forth

TOTAL HEALTH CARE   _____

7. Personal expenses for self

Clothing (include credit card payments) $_____

Dry cleaning   _____

Cosmetics, toiletries   _____

Clubs, recreation   _____

Education   _____

Books, newspapers, magazines, photos   _____

Gifts   _____

Vacations   _____

Other: _____

TOTAL PERSONAL   _____

8. Miscellaneous
     Life insurance $_____
     Court-ordered support or maintenance
         (identify beneficiary of such payment)   _____
     Savings and pension payments   _____
                 TOTAL MISCELLANEOUS   _____
9. Debts not included above

Creditor	Amount	Monthly Payment
_____	_____	_____
_____	_____	_____
_____	_____	_____

          TOTAL MONTHLY DEBT PAYMENTS $_____
10. Total Monthly Expenses (items one
through nine) $_____

PROPERTY: LISTING AND VALUING

The next major area to explore yourself or with your lawyer is property distribution (see chapter seven, "Property Division"). To advise properly the lawyer will need to be adequately informed about *all* of your assets and liabilities. When listing and valuing your property, try to be as specific as possible. The hardest part of this will be placing a valuation on each item. We have included some methods to help you with this task. For example, to find the present market value of your home, enlist the aid of a realtor. He or she will be happy to evaluate your home in the hope of acquiring your listing if you choose to sell. A commonly used source for valuing vehicles is the *N.A.D.A. Official Used Car Guide*, or "blue book," which is published monthly and is available through most automobile dealerships and some public libraries. An insurance adjuster can give you a more accurate value of your car than a car dealership, as they use additional sources for valuing a car, such as the "gold book" and the *Cars of Particular Interest (CPI) Book*. A few telephone calls should give you an idea of the current value of your vehicle, but physical inspection is the only reliable method for determining your car's actual value. The same methods apply to boats and trailers. In some cases you may need to check with your banker or insurance agent.

Property Inventory
1. Family home
   a. Address   _____
      city, state, zip   _____
   b. Date of purchase   _____
   c. Purchase price $_____
   d. Down payment $_____
   e. Source of down payment   _____
   f. Monthly payment $_____
   g. Current mortgage balance $_____
   h. Present market value $_____
   i. Present annual taxes $_____
2. Other (list details as above)
   Vacation property   _____
3. Real estate investment property (raw land, condo, summer
   home, and so forth)
   a. Owned in partnership with   _____
   b. Date of purchase   _____
   c. Purchase price $_____
   d. Down payment $_____
   e. Monthly payments $_____
   f. Taxes $_____
4. Automobiles owned, including motorcycles and recreational
   vehicles

Year	Make	Market Value	Amount Owed	To Whom	Who Uses

5. Boats and trailers

Year	Make	Market Value	Amount Owed	To Whom	Who Uses

6. Furniture and appliances*

Room	Item	Balance Owing	Market Value
		$	$

————	————	————	————
————	————	————	————
————	————	————	————
————	————	————	————
————	————	————	————
————	————	————	————
————	————	————	————
————	————	————	————
————	————	————	————
————	————	————	————
————	————	————	————
————	————	————	————
————	————	————	————
————	————	————	————
————	————	————	————
————	————	————	————
————	————	————	————
————	————	————	————
————	————	————	————
————	————	————	————

*Be sure you do not place too high a value on your home furnishings. A good measure of an item's value is what you would probably get for it at a cash-only garage sale, not the item's retail price or the replacement value.

7. Unusual items—antiques, stamps, coins, sporting equipment, club memberships, other

Item	Date Acquired	Price at Acquisition	Current Market Value	Balance Owed and to Whom	Who uses

8. Life insurance

Face Amount	Company	Type and Number of Policy	Person Insured	Benefits	Cash or Loan Value	Outstanding Loan

9. Bank accounts

Name of Bank	Branch	Type of Account	Current Balance	Who May Withdraw	Name	Date Open

10. Stocks, bonds, commodities, margin accounts

Name	Number of Shares	Purchase Price Per Share	Current Price	Total Current Value	If Bond, List Current Value

11. Certificates of Deposit

	1)	2)	3)
Face amount	_____	_____	_____
Maturity date	_____	_____	_____
Where located	_____	_____	_____
Interest	_____	_____	_____

12. Loans and other debts

	Security Deposits	Earnest Money	Loans	Promissory Notes	Mortgages and Contracts
Amount					
Owed by whom					
Due when					

13. Pension, retirement, profit sharing

	Wife	Husband
a. From whom	_____	_____
b. Your contribution	_____	_____
c. Company contribution	_____	_____
d. State if vested or not	_____	_____
e. If not vested, years to go before vested	_____	_____
f. Lump sum entitled to now	_____	_____
g. Monthly amount entitled to	_____	_____
h. Date and age when entitled	_____	_____
i. Current age	_____	_____

Business valuation: A business may appear to be worth nothing, since almost all profits are consumed by salaries. Salaries do, however, help determine the value of the business. In any event, you will probably need a certified public accountant or an appraiser to find out exactly what the business is worth. The company's most recent financial statements would help this process along.

14. Do you or your spouse own or operate a business?

                                        Yes _____   No _____

    a. Name: _____When started: _____
    b. Were you married then?   Yes _____   No _____
    c. Is it incorporated?   Yes _____   No _____
    d. If yes, total number of shares outstanding: _____
    e. How many shares do you own? _____
    f. How many shares does your spouse own? _____
    g. Are you or your spouse an officer? Yes _____   No _____
      If yes, indicate who and which office: _____
    h. How many employees in business? _____
    i. Net worth (latest quarter or last year): _____
    j. Profit or loss made last year: _____ Last quarter: _____
    k. Where are the books kept? _____

15. Did you help to provide your spouse with an education?

                                        Yes _____   No _____

    (a) If yes, list when: _____
    (b) What education was received? _____
    (c) If you worked then, your monthly take-home pay: _____
    (d) If your spouse worked, his or her monthly take-home
      pay: _____
    (e) The source of each of your incomes:
                  Husband: _____
                  Wife: _____

16. Have you or your spouse completed any financial statements or loan applications?

                                        Yes _____   No _____

Date made: _____
For whom: _____
Present location: _____

17. Have you ever signed an agreement that altered the ownership rights between you and your spouse (for example, a marital or separate property agreement)?

                                        Yes _____   No _____

Date: _____

Where located: _____

Reason for agreement: _____

18. Have you ever signed a guarantee or indemnification agreement, making you or your spouse liable in the event that the other breaches that agreement?

                                     Yes _____   No _____

When signed: _____

For whom: _____

If in default: _____

Amount guaranteed: _____

What security was given? _____

State where agreement located: _____

19. When you married did you give up social security, alimony (maintenance), retirement?

                                     Yes _____   No _____

    a. If yes, list what you gave up: _____

    b. Monthly amount received: _____

    c. How long would you have received it? _____

    d. Can you get it back? _____

20. Separate property: any property that you or your spouse

    a. owned at the time you married: _____

    b. received through inheritance: _____

    c. received as a gift from someone other than spouse: _____

    d. acquired after agreement was executed or divorce action begun: _____

21. If you own such property, list and describe it below:

List Property	Date Acquired	Balance Owed at Time of Marriage	In Whose Name Is Title Held?	How Acquired

22. If you contributed separate property to the marriage, list what property that was, when you contributed it, what the value is, and why you contributed it to the marriage: _____

KEY DOCUMENTS: A CHECKLIST

You should collect photocopies of various documents. As a general rule, all documents that tend to establish ownership of assets, existence of debts, and current income should be assembled and made available. To begin, you should gather the following documents:

1. Federal income tax returns for the last three years.
2. Last three pay stubs for both spouses that show deductions from gross pay.
3. Your current check register (which tends to establish your spending patterns).
4. The most recent annual statement of pension or retirement benefits furnished for each spouse.
5. Savings passbooks.
6. Certificates of deposit, treasury bills, and the like.
7. Financial statements given to a banking institution in connection with a recent loan.
8. Monthly or quarterly bank statements for all checking and savings accounts.
9. Charge card (MasterCard, Visa, American Express, and so forth) statements for the last few months.
10. Warranty deeds, contracts, title insurance, and other documents establishing ownership to real estate, such as your home.
11. Title certificates and registration statements for cars, trucks, recreational vehicles, boats, and so forth.
12. If a business is owned, the most recent tax return, annual profit and loss statement, and most current monthly or quarterly profit and loss statement.
13. List of all current debts, monthly payments, and reason for the debt.
14. Each employer's annual statement describing medical and life insurance benefits, profit sharing plans, and so forth.

The list could go on and on. Use your own common sense to assemble those documents that you feel would be pertinent to defining your financial needs and resources.

FOREIGN CHILD SUPPORT ENFORCEMENT AGENCIES RECIPROCATING WITH THE U.S. GOVERNMENT

CANADIAN PROVINCES

Alberta
Attorney General
Civil Law Section
9833 109th Street
Edmonton, Alberta
Canada T5K 2E8

British Columbia
Attorney General
Parliament Building
850 Burdett Avenue, Fifth Floor
Victoria, British Columbia
Canada V8W L84

Manitoba
Departmental Solicitor
Department of the Attorney General
Woodsworth Building, Sixth Floor
405 Broadway Avenue
Winnipeg, Manitoba
Canada R3C 316

New Brunswick
Registrar's Office
Court of Queen's Bench
Justice Building, Room 201
P.O. Box 6000
Frederickton, New Brunswick
Canada E3B 5H1

Newfoundland/Labrador
Solicitor
Government of Newfoundland and Labrador
Department of Justice
Parliament Building
St. John's, Newfoundland
Canada A1C 517

Nova Scotia
Solicitor
Department of the Attorney General
P.O. Box 7
1723 Hollis Street
Halifax, Nova Scotia
Canada B3J ZL6

Northwest Territories
Commissioner
Government of the Northwest Territories
P.O. Box 1320
Yellowknife, Northwest Territories
Canada XQE 1H0

Ontario
Ministry of the Attorney General
18 King Street East
Toronto, Ontario
Canada M5C 1C5

Prince Edward Island
Attorney General
Parliament Building

Charlottetown, Prince Edward Island
Canada C1A

Quebec
Deputy Attorney General
Ministry of Justice
Government of Quebec
225 E Street
Grand Allee, Quebec
Canada GLR 4C6

Saskatchewan
Attorney General
Province of Saskatchewan
Parliament Building
Regina, Saskatchewan
Canada S4S 0B3

Yukon Territory
Commissioner of the Yukon Territory
Parliament Building
Whitehorse, Yukon Territory
Canada YLA 2C6

UNITED KINGDOM

England and Wales
Home Office
Queen Anne's Gate
London, England SW 1H 9AT

Scotland
Scottish Courts Administration
P.O. Box 37
28 North Bridge
Edinburgh, Scotland EH1 1RA

Northern Ireland
Northern Ireland Courts Service
Courts Business Branch

Windsor House
Bedford Street
Belfast, Northern Ireland 2

OTHER FOREIGN COUNTRIES

Australia
Attorney General's Department
Administrative Building
Parks, Australia
A.C.T. 2600

Bermuda
Administrative Secretary
Deputy Governor's Office
Government House
Bermuda

Fiji
Fiji Mission to the United States
One United Nations Plaza
Twenty-sixth Floor
New York, New York 10017

France
Ministere de la Justice
Bureau de l'Entrade
Judiciare Internationale
13 Place Vendome
75042 Paris, France
Cendex 01

New Zealand
Secretary for Justice
Private Bag, Postal Centre
Wellington, New Zealand

Republic of South Africa
United States Embassy
Thibault House

225 Prestorius Street
Pretoria, Republic of South Africa

Germany
Deutsches Institut fur Vormundschaftswesen
Zahringer Strasse 10
Postfach 102020
69 Heidelberg 1, West Germany

LAWYER REFERRAL SERVICES IN NEW YORK STATE

Statewide
Lawyer Referral and Information Service
New York State Bar Association
Audrey Ryan, Coordinator
One Elk Street
Albany, New York 12207
800-342-3661 (New York State only)
518-463-3200, ext. 2700

Albany County
Lawyer Referral Service
Albany County Bar Association
Barbara Davis, Executive Director
Albany County Courthouse, Room 315
Albany, New York 12207
518-445-7691

Lawyer Referral Service
Capital Chapter Women's Bar
Ava Charne Avellino, Executive Director
P.O. Box 7175
Albany, New York 12224-0175
518-438-5511

Bronx County
Legal Referral Service
Bronx County Bar Association
Mary Conlan, Executive Director
851 Grand Concourse
Bronx, New York 10451
718-293-5600

Broome County
Lawyer Referral Service
Broome County Bar Association
Lorraine Scudder, Administrative Secretary
Bache Building
71 State Street
Binghamton, New York 13901
607-723-6331

Cattaraugus County
Lawyer Referral Service
Cattaraugus County Bar Association
P.O. Box 550
Ellicottville, New York 14731
716-699-8010

Chemung County
Chemung County Human Resource Center
Frank Patterson, Director
425 Pennsylvania Avenue, Room 201
Elmira, New York 14904
607-732-6613

Dutchess County
Lawyer Referral Service
Dutchess County Bar Association
Marie Meehan, Executive Director
P.O. Box 4865
Poughkeepsie, New York 12602
914-473-2488
914-473-7941

Erie County
Lawyer Referral Service
Erie County Bar Association
Carolyn M. Hamele, Coordinator
1360 Statler Building
Buffalo, New York 14202
716-852-3100

Jefferson County
Lawyer Referral Service
Jefferson County Bar Association
Robert Hanrahan, Esq.
161 Clinton Street, Room 204
Watertown, New York 13601
315-782-3520

Kings County
Lawyers' Referral Service
Brooklyn Bar Association
Maxine Donnen, Administrator
123 Remsen Street
Brooklyn, New York 11201
718-624-0843

Monroe County
Lawyer Referral Service
Monroe County Bar Association
Mary Ann Keegan, Esq., Director
39 State Street, Suite 400
Rochester, New York 14614
716-546-2130

Nassau County
Lawyer Referral and Information Service
Nassau County Bar Association
Deborah S. Ferguson, Administrator
Fifteenth and West Streets
Mineola, New York 11501
516-747-4832

New York County
Legal Referral Service
Association of the Bar of the City of New York and New York
County Lawyer Association
Allen J. Charne, Esq., Executive Director
Margaret Sowah, Esq., Assistant Director
42 West 44th Street
New York, New York 10036
212-382-6625

Niagara County
Lawyer Referral Service
Niagara Falls Bar Association
730 Main Street
Niagara Falls, New York 14301
716-282-1242

Onondaga County
Lawyer Reference Service
Onondaga County Bar Association
Helen B. Druce, Executive Director
Marlene LaGrange, LRS Secretary
1000 State Tower Building
Syracuse, New York 13202
315-471-2690

Orange County
Lawyer Referral Service
Orange County Bar Association
Elizabeth Allen, Administrator
P.O. Box 88
Goshen, New York 10924
914-294-8222

Putnam County
Lawyer Referral Service
Putnam County Bar Association
Matthew A. Solano, Chair
Box 44

Carmel, New York 10512
914-225-4904

Queens County
Legal Aid and Referral Service
Queens County Bar Association
Arthur N. Terranova, Esq., Executive Director
90-35 148th Street
Jamaica, New York 11435
718-291-4500

Rensselaer County
Lawyer Referral Service
Rensselaer County Bar Association
John Darling, Esq.
297 River Street
Troy, New York 12180
518-272-7220

Richmond County
Lawyer Referral Service
Richmond County Bar Association
Richard Lasher, Esq., Director
2012 Victory Boulevard
Staten Island, New York 10314-3524
718-442-4500

Rockland County
Lawyer Referral Service
Rockland County Bar Association
Carol Bell, Executive Director
60 South Main Street
New City, New York 10956
914-634-2149

Suffolk County
Lawyer Referral and Information Service
Suffolk County Bar Association
Gabriele K. Wiener, Executive Director
Mary Shannon, LRIS Secretary

340 Veterans Memorial Highway
Commack, New York 11725
516-864-2100

Sullivan County
Lawyer Referral Service
Sullivan County Bar Association
Joseph Jaffe, Vice President, Administration
44 Carrier Street (answering service)
Liberty, New York 12754
914-794-2426

Warren County
Lawyer Referral Service
Warren County Bar Association
Christine Tebbutt, Secretary
Cronin Hi-rise
43 Ridge Street
Glens Falls, New York 12801
518-792-9239

Westchester County
Lawyer Referral Service
Westchester County Bar Association
Gloria A. Willette, Manager
300 Hamilton Avenue, Suite 400
White Plains, New York 10601
914-761-5151

APPENDIX G

---❖---

SUPREME COURTS OF NEW YORK STATE

Albany	Courthouse	Albany	12207	518-487-5019
Allegheny	Courthouse	Belmont	14813	716-268-5800
Bronx	851 Grand Concourse	Bronx	10451	212-590-3717
Broome	Courthouse	Binghamton	13902	607-772-2248
Cattaraugus	303 Court St.	Little Valley	14755	716-938-9111
Cayuga	Courthouse	Auburn	13021	315-253-1400
Chautauqua	P.O. Box 292	Mayville	14757	716-753-4266
Chemung	P.O. Box 588	Elmira	14901	607-737-2847
Chenango	Cnty. Office Bldg.	Norwich	13815	607-335-4573
Clinton	County Government Ctr.	Plattsburg	12901	518-565-4715
Columbia	Courthouse	Hudson	12534	518-828-7858
Cortland	Courthouse	Cortland	13045	607-753-5003
Delaware	P.O. Box 231	Delhi	13753	607-746-2131
Dutchess	Courthouse	Poughkeepsie	12601	914-431-1920
Erie	Erie County Hall	Buffalo	14202	716-851-3291
Essex	County Government Ctr.	Elizabeth Town	12932	518-873-6301
Franklin	Courthouse	Malone	12953	518-483-6767
Fulton	W. Main St.	Johnstown	12095	518-762-0539
Genesee	Courthouse	Batavia	14020	716-344-2550
Greene	Courthouse	Catskill	12414	518-943-2230
Hamilton	Courthouse	Lake Pleasant	12108	518-548-3211
Herkimer	Courthouse	Herkimer	13350	315-867-1186
Jefferson	317 Washington St.	Watertown	13601	315-782-9290
Kings	Montague St.	Brooklyn	11201	718-643-8076
Lewis	Courthouse	Lowville	13367	315-376-5333
Livingston	Courthouse	Geneseo	14454	716-243-7060

Madison	P.O. Box 545	Wampsville	13163	315-366-2267
Monroe	Hall of Justice	Rochester	14614	716-428-5001
Montgomery	Courthouse	Fonda	12068	518-853-4516
Nassau	Supreme Court Bldg.	Mineola	11501	516-535-2966
New York	60 Centre St.	New York City	10007	212-374-8357
Niagara	775 3d St.	Niagara Falls	14302	716-284-3147
Oneida	Courthouse	Utica	13501	315-798-5889
Onondaga	Courthouse	Syracuse	13202	315-425-2030
Ontario	Courthouse	Canandaigua	14424	716-396-4239
Orange	255 Main St.	Goshen	10924	914-294-5151
Orleans	Courthouse	Albion	14411	716-589-5458
Oswego	Courthouse	Oswego	13126	315-342-0025
Otsego	P.O. Box 710	Cooperstown	13326	607-547-4364
Putnam	Courthouse	Carmel	10521	914-225-3641
Queens	88-111 Sutphin Blvd.	Jamaica	11435	718-520-3136
Rensselaer	Courthouse	Troy	12180	518-270-3711
Richmond	County Courthouse	St. George	10301	718-390-5222
Rockland	Courthouse	New City	10956	914-638-5388
St. Lawrence	Courthouse	Canton	13617	315-379-2219
Saratoga	30 McMaster St.	Ballston Spa	12020	518-885-2224
Schenectady	612 State St.	Schenectady	12305	518-388-4250
Schoharie	Courthouse	Schoharie	12157	518-295-8342
Schuyler	Courthouse	Watkins Glen	14891	607-535-7760
Seneca	Courthouse	Waterloo	13165	315-539-7760
Steuben	Putney Sq.	Bath	14810	607-776-7879
Suffolk	235 Griffing Ave.	Riverhead	11901	516-852-2333
Sullivan	Courthouse	Monticello	12701	914-794-4066
Tioga	16 Court St.	Owego	13827	607-687-3133
Tompkins	P.O. Box 70	Ithaca	14850	607-272-0466
Ulster	Courthouse	Kingston	12401	914-339-5680
Warren	County Ctr.	Lake George	12845	518-761-6429
Washington	County Office Bldg.	Fort Edward	12828	518-747-4115
Wayne	Courthouse	Lyons	14489	315-946-5457
Westchester	County Courthouse	White Plains	10601	914-285-4100
Wyoming	143 N. Main St.	Warsaw	14569	716-786-3148
Yates	226 Main St.	Penn Yan	14527	315-536-5129

✦

RESOURCES FOR VICTIMS OF DOMESTIC VIOLENCE

Statewide
New York State Coalition Against Domestic Violence Hotline:
800-942-6906 (English); 800-942-6908 (Spanish)

Directory of New York State Services for Domestic Violence,
published and distributed by:
New York State Coalition Against Domestic Violence
Women's Building
79 Central Avenue
Albany, New York 12206
518-432-4864
There is a $15 charge for the directory.

Brooklyn
Kings County Crisis Center
451 Clarkson Avenue, CG-56C Building
Brooklyn, New York 11203
718-245-3131

Canton
Renewal House
3 Chapel Street
Canton, New York 13617
315-379-9845

Cortland
Aid to Women Victims of Violence
14 Clayton Avenue
Cortland, New York 13045
607-756-6363

Islip Terrace
Long Island Women's Coalition
P.O. Box 183
Islip Terrace, New York 11752
516-666-8833

Ithaca
Task Force for Battered Women
P.O. Box 164
Ithaca, New York 14851
607-277-3203
Twenty-four-hr. crisis hotline: 607-277-5000

Jamaica
Services for the Raped and Battered Victim
90-11 160th Street
Jamaica, New York 11432
718-291-2555

New York City
Victim Service Agency
2 Lafayette Street
New York, New York 10007
212-577-7777
212-274-3209

North Tonawanda
YWCA of the Tonawanda Domestic Violence Program
49 Tremont Street
North Tonawanda, New York 14120
716-692-5643

Plattsburgh
Women Incorporated to Aid, Educate, and Support Women
P.O. Box 44
Plattsburgh, New York 12901
518-563-6904

Queens
Queens Borough Crisis Center
Queens Hospital
82-68 164th Street
Queens, New York 11432
718-318-3819

Rochester
Alternatives for Battered Women
300 Andrews Street
Rochester, New York 14604
716-232-7353

Smithtown
Victim's Information Bureau of Suffolk
496 Smithtown Bypass
Smithtown, New York 11787
516-360-3730

Syracuse
Vera House
P.O. Box 62
Syracuse, New York 13209
315-468-3260

Watertown
Jefferson County Women's Center
52 Public Square
Watertown, New York 13601
315-782-1823

White Plains
Mental Health Association of Westchester County
Abused Spouse Assistance Services
29 Sterling Avenue
White Plains, New York 10606
914-997-1010

Domestic Violence Prosecution Unit
Westchester County DA's Office
110 Grove Street
White Plains, New York 10601
914-285-3000

RECOMMENDED READING ON DIVORCE

Alone: Emotional, Legal, and Financial Help for the Widowed or Divorced Woman, by Antoniak, Scott, and Worcester. A compassionate guide to a difficult period of life.

The Boy's and Girl's Book About Divorce, by Richard Gardner, M.D. The purpose of this book is to help children get along better with their divorced parents. It was written for children ages eight to thirteen and is intended for reading by children alone or with a parent. A parent could read it to younger children ages four to seven. Adolescents, too, will find much of interest to them in this book. Parents often find this book of great help for themselves because it is written from the child's thoughts and feelings.

Boy's and Girl's Book About One-Parent Families, by Richard Gardner, M.D. This book is a warm guide by an excellent author.

Children of Divorce, by J. Louise Despert. This book tells parents in concrete terms how divorce affects children, what to do about it, and where to get help in the doing.

Children's Development During Early Remarriage: The Impact of Divorce, Single-Parenting, and Stepparenting on Children, by J. H. Bray.

Crazy Time: Surviving Divorce, by Abigail Trafford. A focused effort that examines the emotional conflicts faced by males and females during divorce.

Creative Aggression, by Bach and Wyden. A guide to fair fighting.

Creative Divorce, by Mel Krantzler. The focus of this book is on using the crisis of divorce as an opportunity for the growth and development of men and women.

Crisis Time!, by William A. Nolen, M.D. A warm and fascinating autobiography of a successful surgeon who endured a staggering midlife crisis. Dr. Nolen attempts to explain the medical basis for the crisis and offers helpful advice.

"Divorce: A Stress Handbook for Clients," by the Family Law Section, ABA, in *Family Advocate*, Summer 1990.

The Divorced Woman's Handbook, by Jane Wilkie. This book has checklists of things you must do to make it efficiently through the first year after your divorce.

Divorced Women, New Lives, by Ellie Wymard. The author is preparing a second book on the problems of divorced men.

Don't Say Yes When You Want to Say No: Assertiveness Training Book, by Fensterheim and Baer. An excellent workbook for the intimidated spouse.

Explaining Divorce to Children, edited by Earl A. Grollman. Written for parents and professionals as a guidebook explaining the effects of divorce on the personality development of a child, this book will teach you how to talk to children about divorce.

Family Relations Six Years After Divorce, Remarriage, and Stepparenting Today: Research and Theory, by E. M. Hetherington.

A Financial Checklist for Divorce, published by Connecticut Mutual Life Insurance Company, Hartford, Connecticut.

Getting Free, by Ginny NiCarthy, M.S.W. The best book we have found for female victims of emotional and physical abuse. Helpful, nonjudgmental, and empowering.

"Grandparent and Stepparent Rights," by Richard S. Victor, in *Trial Magazine*, 1989: 55–59.

Growing Up with Divorce: Helping Your Child Avoid Immediate and Later Emotional Problems, by Neal Kalter.

The Handbook of Divorce Mediation, by Lenard Marlow and S. Richard Sauber. A comprehensive guide to the issues and processes of divorce mediation.

How to Survive the Loss of a Love, by Melba Colgrove, Ph.D., Harold Bloomfield, M.D., and Peter McWilliams. This book provides many hints about ways to allow you to cope with divorce.

The Impact of Divorce, Single-Parenting, and Stepparenting on Children, by E. M. Hetherington.

Impasses of Divorce, by Johnston and Campbell.

The Intimate Enemy, by Bach and Wyden. A readable guide that examines our fears of intimacy and deep relationships.

Intimate Partners, by Maggie Scarf.

The Kid's Book of Divorce, written by twenty children of divorced families. This book is a child-to-child guide and should be available from your local library.

Living with Loss, by Dr. Ronald W. Ramsay and Rene Noorberger.

Making Contact, by Virginia Satir. A quasi-academic work on establishing or reestablishing relationships with oneself or others.

Male Mid-Life Crisis, by Nancy Mayer. A focused inquiry into problems faced by men in their forties, with helpful suggestions for maintaining relationships while growing.

Man Against Woman: What Every Woman Should Know About Violent Men, by E. Gondolf.

Marital Separation, by Robert Weiss. A classic sociological work. Heavy reading, but worth the effort.

Mom's House, Dad's House, by Isolina Ricci. This book will help parents deal effectively with shared custody.

On Our Own, by John DeFrain, Judy Fricke, and Julie Elman.

Parents Are Forever, booklet published by the Association of Family and Conciliation Courts, Madison, Wisconsin.

Part-Time Father, by Edith Atkin and Estelle Rubin. This book is a guide for the divorced father to help him understand what he will encounter with his children, and how to deal with it.

Passages, by Gail Sheehy. A classic on the life phases of people.

P.E.T. Parent Effectiveness Training, by Thomas Gordon. A simple yet profound guide to parent-child communication.

"Prospective Changes in Marriage, Divorce, and Living Arrangements," by P. C. Glick, in Journal of Family Issues 5 (1984): 7–26.

The Seasons of a Man's Life, by Daniel Levinson. A helpful guide to the life phases faced by men.

Second Chances: Men, Women, and Children a Decade After Divorce, by Judith S. Wallerstein and Sandra Blakeslee.

Separate Houses: A Handbook for Divorced Parents, by Robert B. Shapiro.

Sharing Parenthood After Divorce, by Ciji Ware. An excellent, practical guide to the advantages and disadvantages of shared custody.

Staying Solvent: A Comprehensive Guide to Equal Credit for Women, by Emily Card.

When Parents Divorce: A New Approach to New Relationships, by

Bernard Steinzor. This book will help you deal with the fears and anxieties surrounding the breaking up of a home. Dr. Steinzor shows how today's divorces need no longer be surrounded by hopelessness and a sense of loss—and he means this for both parent and child.

Where Is Daddy? The Story of a Divorce, by Beth Goff. Written for younger children, ages two to five, this is a read-aloud book with lots of drawings. It tells the story of a little girl and what happened to her when her parents divorced and Daddy wasn't there anymore.

Women and Anxiety, by Helen A. DeRosis, M.D. A quasi-academic study, but worth the effort.

Women in Transition: A Feminist Handbook on Separation and Divorce, by Women In Transition, Inc. A very encouraging work.

Your Father's Not Coming Home Any More: Teenagers Tell How They Survive Divorce, by Michael Jackson.

INDEX

247